J. A. Fuller-Maitland

Masters of German Music

J. A. Fuller-Maitland

Masters of German Music

ISBN/EAN: 9783743345867

Manufactured in Europe, USA, Canada, Australia, Japa

Cover: Foto ©Thomas Meinert / pixelio.de

Manufactured and distributed by brebook publishing software (www.brebook.com)

J. A. Fuller-Maitland

Masters of German Music

… asters of Contemporary Music

A SERIES OF BIOGRAPHICAL AND
CRITICAL SKETCHES

Masters of Contemporary Music.

WITH PORTRAITS, &c.

MASTERS OF ENGLISH MUSIC.
By CHARLES WILLEBY,
Crown 8vo, cloth, 5s.

MASTERS OF FRENCH MUSIC.
By ARTHUR HERVEY,
Crown 8vo, cloth, 5s.

Frontispiece

Masters of German Music

BY
J. A. FULLER MAITLAND

WITH ILLUSTRATIONS

LONDON
OSGOOD, McILVAINE & CO.
45 ALBEMARLE STREET
1894

DEDICATED

BY GRACIOUS PERMISSION

TO

HER ROYAL HIGHNESS

PRINCESS CHRISTAN

OF SCHLESWIG-HOLSTEIN

PRINCESS HELENA

OF GREAT BRITAIN AND IRELAND

PREFACE

For much of the material of this book *I am* indebted, not only to several of the composers themselves, who have kindly given information not otherwise obtainable, but to G. J. Bennett, Esq., Mus. D.; G. Milner-Gibson-Cullum, Esq.; W. Ashton Ellis, Esq.; Frau Dr. Kilian, of Dresden; H. E. Rensburg, Esq.; Miss Eugenie Schumann; Mr. and Mrs. W. Shakespeare; Messrs. Simrock; Edward Speyer, Esq., and in particular to R. H. Legge, Esq., who has given me invaluable assistance *in every part of the work.*

J. A. FULLER MAITLAND.

London, 1894.

CONTENTS

	PAGE
JOHANNES BRAHMS	1
MAX BRUCH	97
KARL GOLDMARK	137
JOSEF RHEINBERGER	173
THEODOR KIRCHNER—CARL REINECKE—WOLDEMAR BARGIEL	199
JOSEPH JOACHIM—CLARA SCHUMANN	217
HEINRICH VON HERZOGENBERG—HEINRICH HOFMANN—ANTON BRUCKNER—FELIX DRAESEKE	237
JEAN LOUIS NICODÉ—RICHARD STRAUSS—HANS SOMMER—CYRILL KISTLER	263

LIST OF ILLUSTRATIONS

JOHANNES BRAHMS		*Frontispiece*
FRAGMENT OF SONG "MAGYARISCH" BY BRAHMS		*To face p.* 28
AUTOGRAPH CANON BY BRAHMS HITHERTO UNPUBLISHED	,,	80
MAX BRUCH	,,	97
FACSIMILE OF AUTOGRAPH SCORE BY MAX BRUCH	,,	117
KARL GOLDMARK	,,	137
FACSIMILE OF AUTOGRAPH SCORE BY KARL GOLDMARK	,,	158
JOSEF RHEINBERGER	,,	173
FACSIMILE OF AUTOGRAPH SCORE BY JOSEF RHEINBERGER	,,	184

JOHANNES BRAHMS

LITTLE more than a decade since, the musical world of Germany was dominated by two men who divided between them the allegiance of the intelligent musicians of the Fatherland. If you were not among the Wagnerians you were by that fact enrolled among the partisans of Brahms; to appreciate neither master was to own yourself a hopeless Philistine, but to profess an admiration for both was to adopt a position which was obviously untenable. The war was not the less keenly carried on because there were no such scenes as made memorable the battle of the Gluckists and Piccinists, or that of the admirers of Faustina and Cuzzoni. Every sort of invective and misrepresentation was employed by the journalists who fought in the front ranks of the action, and no doubt some ingenious person will one day collect from the Wagnerian literature a companion volume to the famous dictionary of opprobrious epithets applied to the Bayreuth master by his opponents. It should be clearly understood that the question at issue was chiefly the position of Wagner; the parties were rightly described as Wagnerians and anti-Wagnerians, not as Brahmsians and anti-Brahmsians or even as Wagnerians and Brahmsians. But the composer to whom the most influential and intelligent of the anti-Wagnerian party have looked to counteract the tendencies of "the music of the future," and to continue the great line of German composers, has of course been forced into a prominent position in the combat, even though his personal share in the quarrel has been of the slightest.

Since the death of Wagner left only one composer of the highest rank at the head of German musicians, there has gradually sprung up a feeling of toleration on each side, not for the other, but for those who can conscientiously claim to be numbered among the admirers of both the great masters of the latter half of the nineteenth century. And it is absurd to suppose that mankind can persist in ignoring one of two things—either the poetic imagination and dramatic power of the creator of the "music drama," or the freedom, originality, and constructive genius of the present representative of the classical masters. Part of the great debt which English lovers of modern music owe to Hans Richter is on account of his having placed, from the beginning of his concerts in London, the works of Brahms and Wagner side by side in positions of equal honour. His doing so has undoubtedly enabled English musicians to free themselves from the prejudices to which too many Germans are still subject. As an instance of how little the German condition of things can be paralleled among ourselves, the remark of an eminent and somewhat self-centred English musician may be quoted, who, on hearing of a new appointment on the musical press, observed: "—— is a dangerous man; he is an admirer of Brahms and Wagner." One can hardly conceive the remark being made by even the most *borné* of German musicians.

It is not necessary to go into the Wagner controversy, except for the sake of illustrating the position held by Brahms in the musical world of Germany at the present time. In their desire to bring forward a champion in opposition to Wagner, the antagonists of the modern developments of the art could find no composer but Brahms worthy of the place. In fact no attempt was made on behalf of any other musician, and both sides accepted him as the defender of musical orthodoxy. Of course a position of this kind, or even one of absolute pre-eminence, is not any sort of actual criterion of greatness. In England, as everywhere else, sensible men know how little the public estimate in such matters is really worth; but Germany at the present moment affords a striking instance of the coincidence of popular and expert valuation. And it is impossible to study the compositions of Brahms as a whole and not to realise that their author is one of the strongest personalities in the whole line of the masters of music. If evidence of this were wanting from without, we have only to consider the hostility with which they are still received in some quarters; for the existence of a strong opposition implies strength in the thing opposed. Relatively to his contemporaries, he stands on so great a height that it is difficult to see how the great line of German composers is to be maintained after him. He is of an age when his successor should be already in active work in the world of music, but as yet no one has appeared who promises to succeed him worthily, and it would almost seem as if the tide of music, which for so many years has favoured Germany above all other nations, were at the ebb at last. If it is fated to be so, and Germany is to become a second-rate power in art, it will be interesting to see which of the nations will succeed her in the supremacy. France has long had a fine school of earnest and accomplished composers; if the younger Italians will follow the noble example set them by their oldest composer, they may reach the high place that once belonged to their countrymen by a kind of natural heritage; and a wave of music has lately been passing over England which may bring about a condition of things only to be compared with the glorious days when England was the chief among musical nations. We have not to deal, however, with the future, but with the present state of music in Germany, and with its greatest representative there.

It is difficult to see what quality of greatness is absent from this composer's work; the grandeur, wealth, and originality of his ideas, and the ease and power with which he uses forms already invented, or develops them into new organisms full of suggestion and opportunity for those who may come after, are, perhaps, the most striking of his peculiar attributes; but there is also a **deep expression as well as an** exquisite beauty in the greatest **of his works.** He is sometimes accused of **neglecting the** merely pleasing side of **music, and,** as far as some of his earlier compositions are concerned, it is certainly possible to find passages where sensuous beauty of melody is not easily to be **discovered.** Taking the whole of his work into **consideration, however, it** is quite impossible to **agree with the charge, for** no composer, past or present, has invented lovelier **melodies, or** has set them in more delightful surroundings; and they are to be found in nearly all his works, scattered through them with no niggard hand. Of course, if the only function of music is to appeal to the lower emotions of the less cultivated classes, then Brahms cannot rank with the great masters at all; **but in that** case the whole **of musical** history **must be** re-arranged, and Beethoven must be recognised as the artistic inferior of Offenbach or the compiler of the last street song. Where the usual tests of musical **merit** are fairly applied, there must Brahms rank **with** the masters of the first order. **There is one test** which it is a **little dangerous to apply, since it takes from certain popular idols their long-held position of supremacy: it can only be** of real value when all allowances are made for circumstances and the influence of the outer world upon the artist's life. It is the test that is applied to a chain, the strength of which is judged by that of its weakest link; in matters of art it resolves itself into the question, "Does a man's work contain examples altogether unworthy of himself at his best?" This does not, of course, imply a dead level throughout his work, for such a level must be one of mediocrity; but it requires the absence of any composition obviously written to order or against the grain, or of anything the composer would be ashamed of in his better moments. We need not take into account the posthumous compositions of any master, for these may be merely the contents of his waste-paper basket, thrust into publicity by injudicious survivors; but the Devil's Advocate will have to expel many a famous name from the list of the supreme masters, and in fact, putting aside the old composers, whose weaker works may very likely have disappeared, there will remain few beside Bach, Beethoven, Schumann, and, curiously enough, Chopin. In the case of Mozart and Haydn, it must be remembered that the condition of the musical world in their day made it imperative upon them to write in and out of season. This high test, it is not too much to say, is fulfilled by one living composer alone, and his name is JOHANNES BRAHMS. Through the long list of his works we may search in vain for music that he need blush to own; naturally some are far better than others, but in the least attractive we shall find signs of the master's genius, whether in the manipulation of an unpromising theme or the exact portrayal of some subtlety of expression. The felicitous combination of intense earnestness of aim and nobility of ideal with the passionate ardour that is characteristic of Southern countries, may well have its origin in the circumstances of his life: the first possibly comes from his North German birth, the second from the artistic atmosphere of Vienna, the city of his adoption.

Johannes Brahms was musical by inheritance; his father, a double-bass player in the opera band at Hamburg, was also a proficient on other instruments, and the boy, born May 7, 1833, was put, at a very early age, under the tuition of a pianoforte-teacher named Gossel. Eduard Marxsen of Altona has the honour of being named as the young composer's principal teacher, and his complete theoretical equipment, his refined taste, and great experience as a teacher, were invaluable in directing the genius of his pupil into the highest paths. At fourteen years of age, Brahms gave a concert or "piano-recital," at which a set of variations on a Volkslied was brought forward as an example of his creative power. Most fortunately for him and for his art, he was not forced into the career of a pianoforte prodigy; no doubt this was due partly to Marxsen's good sense and the parents' wisdom, but it is also possible that the amount of actual "virtuosity" displayed by the boy was not so exceptional as to make it advisable from a commercial point of view. In later life, the composer's playing has been described as possessing an amount of interest and beauty all its own: in particular, his performance of Bach's organ works on the piano is said to be quite phenomenal, and of his playing in general it has been said that it is "powerful and soft, full of pith and meaning, and never louder than it is lovely." Still, the qualities that are essential in a successful performer, such as brilliancy and perfect technical accuracy, are not among the attractions mentioned by those who have been privileged to hear him play. Even in Germany, where we are accustomed to think of musical skill always and at once receiving its due reward, young composers cannot immediately make a living by their works, and an association with Remenyi, a Hungarian violinist who has already almost outlived the great reputation he once enjoyed, had an influence on Brahms' career which could not have been foreseen. While acting as this artist's accompanist on a concert tour in 1853 he came across Joachim and Liszt, the former of whom was destined to become one of his most intimate friends and keenest admirers. It may easily be imagined how great was the influence exerted by the illustrious violinist, who was also an artist of the most earnest purpose, upon the young composer, to whom the companionship of a mere virtuoso must have been far from satisfying. We have only to look at the list of Brahms' works to see how many and how important are the results of the intimacy which now began; for it is no secret that some of the most beautiful and popular of these compositions were primarily intended for Joachim, and first played by him. Joachim was nearly two years the older of the pair, and by this time had already made an European fame for himself. It was no doubt a thing quite outside his previous experience to find a pianist who could at a moment's notice transpose the piano part of the "Kreutzer sonata" from A to B flat when he found that the pianoforte was half a tone flat; and it was not every day that he met with a composer or a composition student, who had already finished a group of works so original and full of promise as the pianoforte sonatas, the scherzo in E flat minor, and the first set of songs. That he should give the young man a letter of introduction to Schumann, who was then living at Düsseldorf, was almost a matter of course, since Schumann was always eager to hear of new writers or musicians of any kind who were really in earnest. When we consider these earliest achievements of Brahms' genius, it will not seem surprising that Schumann should have taken up his pen, which had been long idle, in eloquent praise of the newcomer.

The sonata in C, op. 1, has for the principal subject of its first movement a theme almost identical with that of Beethoven's great sonata in B flat, op. 106. The resemblance *saute aux yeux*, and has not escaped the notice of the German biographers of the master; but it throws into all the greater prominence the astonishing originality of its treatment. The slow movement, built upon the theme of a national song, is an early example of the composer's fondness for characteristic traditional melodies, and the coda of the movement is of magical beauty. The second sonata, in F sharp minor, has much originality of design, exhibited in the employment of the same subject for the slow movement and the scherzo, and the expressive recurrence of the introduction to the finale at its close. The third, in F minor, op. 5, must almost have been the piece about which a story is told, to the effect that when an admirer ventured to point out some reminiscence of Mendelssohn, the composer remarked rather grumpily (as well he might): "True, such things will happen sometimes, even to the best of us; the pity only is that every donkey should go and find it out at once!" The story is told of a new concerted piece of his later period, but as this sonata is the only instance of Mendelssohn's influence on the composer, I may perhaps be forgiven for surmising that it belongs to the earlier work. The beautiful resumption of the slow movement called "Rückblick," and the exquisite subsidiary theme of the finale, a chorale-like subject in D flat, are enough to distinguish the sonata. The scherzo, op. 4, was sufficiently in the vein of a more vigorous Chopin to excite the admiration of Liszt, an admiration which was bestowed on very few other works by Brahms. Perhaps the most surprising thing in this first batch of compositions is the very first song of the group numbered op. 3, the powerful ballad "Liebestreu," beginning "O versenk!" The setting of each stanza is the same, it is true, and it is perhaps unlikely that in his maturer years Brahms would have been content to leave it so; but the steady increase in dramatic passion is actually intensified by the fact that the change is only made in speed and tone-colour. Surely no first-fruits of genius were ever more strikingly individual than these, or contained things of greater promise. If Schumann's experienced eye could detect, as it undoubtedly did, the future characteristics of a Chopin in the conventional set of variations on "La ci darem," he had an easier task here, and the different tone of his famous article, "Neue Bahnen," marks his sense of the greatness of the career he foresaw. In this remarkable article the young composer is greeted as "one who should claim the mastership by no gradual development, but burst upon us fully equipped, as Minerva sprang from the brain of Jupiter." In one respect alone was Schumann wrong in his prophecy—that there was to be no further development in Brahms' powers. It is no doubt true that he has undergone no great revolution of convictions or of style, and that the earliest and latest of his works have possibly more in common with each other than the corresponding works of any other composer whatever; but at the same time an unmistakable tendency has shown itself in his later years towards clearness of utterance and the abandonment of many of the characteristics that were least pleasing to superficial hearers. Not that his thoughts are less deep now than they were when they were harder to understand, but they are more clearly and directly enunciated, more flowing in their treatment, and therefore more agreeable to those who do not care to go beneath the surface. For those who do care to go deeper, and who are, therefore, capable of the highest degree of musical enjoyment, the later works are not less, but more, full of interest, than the earlier. Looking back upon this first group of works, they afford an interesting parallel with those of Beethoven, for, like them, they are influenced by the composer's predecessors, while they contain unmistakable tokens of strong individuality. In the same group as the compositions just referred to falls the first of the master's trios for piano and strings, the work in B major, op. 8, which was published about the same time as the sonatas and three books of songs. This trio has lately acquired an interest and importance beyond almost any other work of the composer's, since a few years ago he remodelled it, and a comparison of the two versions is an invaluable lesson in composition, as well as an incident scarcely to be paralleled in musical history. It is the best proof that can be given of what was asserted above—that an exceptional degree of unity in style has always subsisted between the earlier and the later compositions of Brahms. For though a period of nearly forty years divides the two versions, the latter, which contains very little material that is actually new, has no lack of homogeneity, although in every movement important alterations have been made. As a rule these are in the direction of making the general course of the work clearer and more intelligible; in its earlier form it was one of the most difficult of his works, not only to play, but to understand. One of the changes demonstrates an amount of self-criticism that is the rarest of all virtues among artists of all kinds. In the adagio there occurred a theme of beautifully melodious character, exactly suiting its place as a contrasting subject to the main theme, but, unfortunately, very strongly resembling the opening of Schubert's song, "Am Meer." This has now been replaced by a long-drawn theme in G sharp minor, given out by the violoncello. But it would take too long to enumerate the alterations and the reasons for each, though a more profitable exercise can hardly be recommended to young composers.

In 1854 Brahms stayed for some time with Liszt at Weimar, and appeared on several occasions as a pianist at Hanover, for this career had not been definitely given up at that time; the post of choir-director and music-master to the Prince of Lippe-Detmold, to which he was appointed about the same time, gave him occupation of a more or less lucrative kind during the winter months, and plenty of opportunity for the quiet development of his powers, for which, of course, no help from other composers was any longer necessary. It would be an interesting study for the musical historian to estimate the influence of these posts at the small German Courts upon German music. Not merely the leisure for composition, the various opportunities for performance of the composer's efforts, have to be considered, but the familiarity with practical music—in this case with a choir—and, last but not least, the intercourse with cultivated people. A long period of service in this sort of capacity would inevitably lead, however, to a gradual merging of the artist in the pedant, and it was to Brahms' advantage that he gave up the post after a few years, and returned to Hamburg, subsequently living for a time in Switzerland, where he enjoyed the friendship, sympathy, and good advice of Theodor Kirchner. His appearance at one of the Gewandhaus concerts in conservative Leipzig, in January 1859, in his own pianoforte concerto, op. 15, was not successful; for this the notorious reluctance of the audience to accept anything really new cannot be held wholly responsible, since the concerto is one of the least attractive of the composer's works, exhibiting all the harshnesses of his early manner in an excessive degree. At the same time it is interesting to notice how even here is to be traced a characteristic of all the master's work in this kind, the complete blending of the solo part with the orchestral, so that each part exists for the sake, not of itself, but of the whole. When it appeared in print, in the early sixties, it was in the same group with some compositions that have enjoyed immediate and almost universal popularity from the date of their first performance until the present day. The two serenades (op. 11 and 16, in D and A respectively) are less often given in England than the lovely sextet in B flat for strings, op. 18, but they are not less beautiful; and the wonderful and, as it has been called, Haydnesque, clearness of structure which now begins to distinguish the composer's best works, is all the more remarkable when compared with the qualities of the piano concerto. An "Ave Maria" for female chorus, orchestra and organ (op. 12), a funeral hymn for chorus and wind instruments (op. 13), and a group of part-songs or trios for female voices accompanied by two horns and harp (op. 17) show that at this time the composer was making experiments in tone-colour; the last is especially successful, and it is curious to note how happy the composer has always been in dealing with the horn, whether in the larger or the smaller combinations.

Though many of these works have precisely the characteristics that were ascribed, a little while ago, to the influence of the Austrian capital, Brahms did not take up his residence in Vienna until after they were not only written, but actually published. It was in 1862 that he appeared there, and gave a number of pianoforte recitals to the delight of the more cultivated Viennese musicians. Within a year from his arrival he was appointed director of the Singakademie; but resigned it after a year of useful work, devoted in large measure to the study of Bach's choral music. For some three years he had no fixed place of abode, but visited various towns for short periods. He conducted the first serenade at Cologne (where he had, years before, been offered a post in the Conservatorium, but had refused it), and gave concerts in Switzerland. In 1867 he returned to Vienna, which has since been his head quarters.

The artistic result of these "Wanderjähre" was a most important group of chamber-compositions, including the two delightful quartets for piano and strings (op. 25 and 26, in G minor and A respectively), the splendid quintet in F minor (op. 34), the second sextet in G (op. 36,) the sonata for piano and violoncello (op. 38), and the lovely "horn" trio in E flat (op. 40)—truly, a batch of compositions that might have set up two or three composers in the estimation of musicians! In the finale of the first of these, the wonderful "Gipsy rondo" of the G minor quartet, we have the most important example of that love of Hungarian colouring and themes which, in connection with the well-known arrangements of the "czardas" for pianoforte duet, did so much to make Brahms' name familiar to English amateurs. The exquisite tone-colour of the slow movement of the other quartet is not less worthy of remark, and these two works and the quintet are among the loveliest of the master's works. Another beautiful instance of Magyar characteristics is a set of variations upon a Hungarian song, for piano, op. 21a, the theme of which has a curious rhythm of seven crotchets disposed in two bars, that reappears in the slow movement of the latest of his pianoforte trios. The variation form occupied the composer much at this time; not only was there a very beautiful companion set to that already mentioned, but a four-hand set on a theme by Schumann, a solo set (culminating in a masterly fugue) on a theme from one of the less familiar harpsichord suites of Handel, and a set of twenty-eight enormously difficult studies in the form of variations on a theme by Paganini, date from the same period, the earliest of the composer's maturity. In two other branches of composition the same group contains work of importance; the set of nine songs to words by A. von Platen and G. F. Daumer, containing the exquisite lyric, "Wie bist du, meine Königin?" and the great set of fifteen romances from Tieck's "Magelone," are unsurpassed in beauty and tenderness of expression by any of his later songs, and in them is reached the highest point of development of the German "Lied."

The chief interest of certain sacred choral works, such as Psalm xiii. for female choir and organ, the setting of Flemming's "Lass dich nur nichts dauern," and others, is in the fact that they are practically sketches for the most famous of Brahms' contributions to sacred music, the "German Requiem." In the sketches a most noble dignity and gravity is maintained, while every sort of contrapuntal device is to be found in them, though these are in no sense obtruded upon the hearer's notice. The two works mentioned, as well as the two motets for five-part chorus, unaccompanied, of which the vigorous " Es ist das Heil " is the better known, in England at least, are in the finest style of church music—broad, dignified, and wholly free from sentimentality. As an illustration of the composer's industry in the production of choral music just at this time, it may be worth mentioning that this branch of art is represented in this period by no less than seven opus-numbers in the catalogue, some of them including as many as five compositions.

The work for which these were in a sense preparatory studies is, it is not too much to say, the greatest achievement of modern sacred music in Germany. It was possibly suggested by the Austrian and Prussian war of 1866, but a more personal element seems gradually to have obtruded itself. It is curious that it should have been at first performed piecemeal, the first three choruses under Herbeck in 1867, and six out of the seven numbers in 1868 at Bremen: the reason for this was simply that the oratorio as we now have it was not finished until later in 1868. The scheme lent itself to gradual enlargement, for the words chosen from

JOHANNES BRAHMS

Scripture by the composer himself do not follow in any very necessary sequence. The title is a little clumsy, for there is nothing whatever in common with the Requiem of the Catholic ritual, and there is nothing essentially German in the passages selected or in their treatment, except that they are taken from the Lutheran Bible. Without touching further upon the composer's religious beliefs, it is quite clear, from the way in which the different texts are strung together and from the depth of devotional expression revealed in almost every number, that Brahms must, at the time of its composition, have been under strong religious impressions. Not Bach himself has penetrated more deeply into the spiritual meaning of the thoughts called up by the death of one beloved, though the distinctively "pietistic" element of his church cantatas and the like is not forthcoming in the newer composition. The first chorus opens with the calm utterance of the words "Blessed are they that mourn," succeeded by the promise "They that sow in tears shall reap in joy," set to music of the most consolatory character imaginable. With the second number we enter upon the contemplation of the "four last things," which, it may be, would have suggested the title for the work, if the equivalent of this name had not already been appropriated by Spohr in the work which we in England know as "The Last Judgment." The idea of the whole human race marching in solemn procession to the grave, is one that on two separate occasions inspired no less prosaic a person than Dr. Watts to genuine poetic utterance; in Blake's wonderful illustrations to Young's "Night Thoughts" there is a design, among many others that haunt the memory, representing Time as sitting beside a river in the stream of which are borne along types of every age and condition of mankind on their way to death. The same idea inspired Brahms to the composition of a march unlike all marches that ever were written, but not to be mistaken by the most superficial hearer for anything but a march. It is in *triple time*, and in this, and in the inevitable character of the music, we know that we are listening to the tramp of no ordinary host. The effect is heightened by the employment of unisons in the vocal parts, which seem to give the sense of chill helplessness as the words are sung "Behold, all flesh is as the grass." The imagery of the words, perhaps connected with the "sowing in tears" of the previous chorus, suggests the passage from the Epistle of St. James, "The husbandman waiteth for the precious fruit of the earth," and this leads by no abrupt transition to the beautiful fugal setting of the familiar words, "The redeemed of the Lord shall return." The reiteration of the words "joy everlasting," with which the chorus closes, is a most striking contrast to the gloom of the beginning. A somewhat analogous principle of construction underlies the next number, yet the treatment is so vastly different that no sense of repetition is created. It starts with a baritone solo, " Lord, make me to know mine end," melodious, expressive, and pre-eminently vocal; a passage of fine suggestion, at the words " My hope is in Thee," in which the four sections of the choir, entering successively from the lowest register of the bass to the high soprano, give the idea of a hope built upon a sure foundation, leads into the splendid fugue throughout on a "pedal point," "But the righteous souls are in the hands of God," in which the same impression of stability and permanence is admirably conveyed. If any doubt existed as to the greatness and originality of this creation, it received the crowning testimony to its power in the disapproval it excited among the German pundits of the time, who were naturally blind to its emotional meaning, and only saw in it a bold innovation on their jealously-guarded fugue-form. After the assurance as to the destiny of the "righteous souls" it is natural to turn to the celestial joys of their abode, and in the next number, "How lovely is Thy dwelling-place!" the perfect peace of heaven is reflected, and the longing of the faithful heart for the Beatific Vision. The subject of the next number, that of comfort to mourners, based upon the happy state of the holy dead, follows so naturally what has gone before that it is difficult to believe it to have been composed later than all the rest. A personal loss, that of the composer's mother, is said to have determined its form, which is that of a soprano solo, kept for the most part in its high register, and accompanied by a quiet choral section, which repeats the words, "As one whom his own mother comforteth, so will I comfort you." The solo part may be open to the reproach of not being very easy to sing—an unpardonable sin in the eyes of many English amateurs—but of its real effect and profoundly impressive character in the hands of a competent artist there can be no manner of doubt. The sixth chorus really deserves the epithet "monumental," so often misapplied by German and English critics. Beginning with a passage of simple four-part harmony, "Here we have no continuing place," the composer leads our thoughts towards that change from mortality to immortality on which the Lutheran, like the Anglican, burial-service lays stress. To English amateurs, saturated with "The Messiah" from their earliest youth, there may well have seemed something almost sacrilegious in re-setting the words, "For the trumpet shall sound," etc., and giving them to a baritone soloist; but even if the resemblance to Handel's work went farther than it does, we must remember that the oratorio in which the familiar air occurs is far less often given, and far less universally adored, in Germany than here. The "mystery," described in wonderfully graphic strains, though by the simplest means imaginable, is represented in the chorus parts by a vigorous and well-developed section in triple time, "For the trumpet shall sound," in which, for once, the element of dramatic excitement is allowed to appear, though only as a preparation for the calm dignity and devotional grandeur of the magnificent double fugue, "Lord, Thou art worthy." After this surprising peroration, in order to bring back the prevailing tone of the Requiem, the final number, modelled more or less closely upon the first, resumes the thoughts connected with the departed, and closes in undoubtedly more appropriate expression than if the penultimate chorus, with its jubilant outburst of praise, had been allowed to end the work.

While preparing this work for the press, in the summer of 1868, Brahms stayed at Bonn, where he wrote also a large number of songs and two important works for male choir and orchestra, each with a part for a solo voice; the first of these, "Rinaldo" (op. 50), in which a tenor soloist is employed, is set to Goethe's adaptation from Tasso, and is conceived in the finest spirit of romance; the second, "Rhapsodie" (op. 53), set to a passage from the same poet's "Harzreise im Winter," contains a part for alto or mezzo-soprano, and the strange and beautiful effects due to the unusual combination of voices entitle the work to more general recognition than it has yet received, even if it were not one of the most melodious and impressive of the larger works of the master. The smooth, sustained passage,

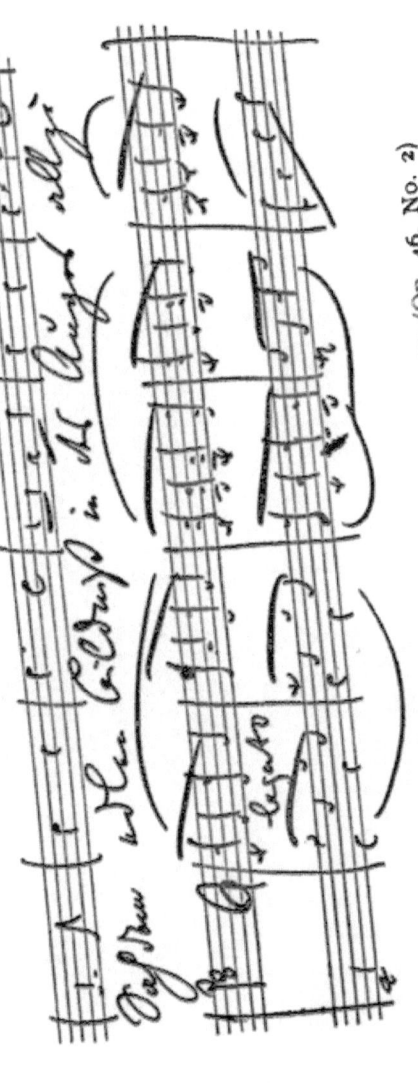

FRAGMENT OF SONG "MAGYARISCH" BY BRAHMS (Op. 46, No. 2)

Inserted by kind permission of E. Speyer, Esq., and Messrs. Simrock, the owners respectively of the autograph and the copyright of the song.

"Ist auf deinem Psalter, Vater der Liebe," has a haunting loveliness that is not easily forgotten. In strong contrast with these and the Requiem is one of the works produced about this time, which may perhaps be regarded as the healthy natural reaction after the continued concentration on the solemn subject of the Requiem: the famous "Liebeslieder-Walzer," op. 52, though written away from Vienna, may well have been a reflection of the most characteristic popular music of the Austrian capital and the performances of Strauss' band in the Volksgarten, which have been among Brahms' most constant enjoyments since his first visit to that city of pleasure. In the waltzes written some time before for piano duet, op. 39, Brahms showed how much of real emotion could be put into the conventional form, without straining it, as Schumann often did in his adaptations of the waltz to romantic music. Here the piano duet is again employed, but in association with four solo voices, a combination which Schumann was the first to use in his "Spanische Liebeslieder." Brahms' waltzes are short, and adhere most strictly to the prescribed structure: this is, of course, simplicity itself, yet we never feel that the great composer is conscious of any want of freedom. He yields himself up unrestrainedly to the mood of the dancers, for whom we may imagine the waltzes to be intended—for many of them could perfectly well serve for the practical purposes of the ball-room. The people who are fond of complaining that there is so little of what they call "tune" in Brahms' music, should turn their attention to these waltzes, and the later series, op. 65. By "tune" they mean, as is well known, melody cut into lengths of exactly eight bars, neither more nor less; of the character of the melody they take little notice, and they will rave about quite ugly music, provided only it has "tunes" in this sense. Here they will find a wealth of such tunes, cut into lengths as definite as the latest English royalty ballad, though a good deal less threadbare in the quality of the music. While the less cultivated amateur may enjoy the waltzes in his own way, the musician wonders at the skill with which the vocal and instrumental parts are interwoven, and at the amount of interest and real value the pieces have, for all their popular guise. In the earlier set there is no such deeply poetic "envoy" as is attached to the later series, "Nun, ihr Musen, genug" —one of the most beautiful musical inspirations in existence; but in spite of this, there is plenty of romantic sentiment and playful humour to be found in them, and their enormous popularity need not be wondered at. The fate of the second series, in England at least, is widely different from that which befalls most sequels, since it is more admired, or at all events more often given, than the first. It may not be useless to draw attention to the wording of the title, which gives the most excellent hint as to the secret of obtaining a good performance. The waltzes are not described as "quartets with four-hand piano accompaniment," but as duets with four voices *ad libitum*. The singers must follow, not lead, the players, if an effective rendering is to be given; of course the latter must make allowance for the presence of the vocal parts, but they must not hesitate to adopt the thousand little modifications of time that are suggested by the instrumental phrases, as they might well do if the pianoforte were used simply as an accompaniment. In both sets of waltzes, and in other works of kindred arrangement, a peculiar charm is felt, and the actual treatment of the voice-parts has an individuality that is difficult to analyse.

The German victories of 1870–1 were celebrated in a noble "Triumphlied," op. 55, for baritone solo, eight-part chorus, and orchestra, first performed at Bremen on Good Friday, 1871. It is a little strange that it is not oftener given at English festivals, since our own national anthem, long since adapted by the Germans as "Heil dir im Siegerkranz," appears in a much disguised form in its first number, and the chorale, "Nun danket Alle Gott"—a hymn-tune scarcely less familiar here than in its native land—is referred to in its second. Next to this in order of composition comes a very famous specimen of Brahms' skill in choral writing, the picturesque and suggestive "Schicksalslied," or song of destiny (op. 54), which, in its moderate extent and real effectiveness seems to have set the pattern for those shorter choral works in which some of the best of our living English composers have expressed themselves most successfully. In the poetic depth of emotion, in the contrast between its two sections, and in the hopeful teaching of the music, as against the fatalistic purport of the words, we are here conscious, as before in the Requiem, that the author has entered into the very soul of his subject, and that he is no mere machine for setting words to suitable music. The opening section describes the state of

Olympian calm in which the pagan deities may be supposed to pass an eternity of unruffled happiness. The pure beauty of the music in this part is greatly enhanced by the fine orchestration, and the movement gives place all too soon to a rapid and restless section in triple time, in which the harsh destiny of the human race is considered. As in the second number of the Requiem, the choral parts sweep to and fro as though driven before a resistless tempest. Hölderlin's line "Wie Wasser von Klippe zu Klippe geworfen" is set to a most graphic passage of staccato notes in cross rhythm, and the final words of the poem "Ins Ungewisse hinab" suggest a headlong falling into non-existence, illustrated in the gradual dying away of the voices in their lowest registers. Here is where the composer asserts his own individuality, for the work does not end at this point; in an instrumental epilogue, built on the theme of the quiet opening, he seems to show us that there is a hope beyond the poet's ken, that the pessimistic view of life may not perhaps be the true one after all. The power of instrumental music to suggest definite non-musical ideas—that power generally denied by the partisans of what is called "absolute" music, among whom

Brahms is usually counted—was never better illustrated.

By this time the composer had finally fixed upon Vienna as his permanent home, and had even accepted new duties connected with the performance of music, having been appointed conductor of the famous concerts of the "Gesellschaft der Musikfreunde," a post which he filled with much success until 1875, when he resigned it to his friend Herbeck. From this time forth, a period now of nearly twenty years, he has devoted himself exclusively to composition, in surroundings the most congenial that can be imagined, and, as far as can be known, his life is arranged almost ideally for the production of artistic work of the finest kind. He is no example of the prosperous musician who is contented to receive the homage of the world, and to give it in return his less happily inspired effusions. Nor need we fear his becoming the centre of a mutual admiration society, or turning into a narrow-minded pedant, such as are not unknown among German and English musicians. Power such as he possesses is its own safeguard, and all that it requires for its full development is freedom from outward vexations, though indeed

JOHANNES BRAHMS

Beethoven's powers are not held to have been lessened by either of the two trials of his latter days, his ne'er-do-weel nephew and his deafness. Brahms, though happily free from such troubles, stands in little danger of being "spoilt," for yet another reason, which is a certain most salutary intolerance of anything like the "lionising" process; at no time has his manner to strangers or mere acquaintances been remarkable for urbanity, but on the slightest suspicion of expressed admiration he assumes a stony or rather thorny impenetrability, and many an ardent and too outspoken amateur has had reason to regret his boldness. Like Tennyson and many another son of the muses, he is bored to death with that kind of thing, and does not scruple to show it. There is a story—only one of many—that illustrates this peculiarity particularly well, though it may not exhibit the master in a very amiable light. At Baden-Baden, where he often passes part of the summer, he was accosted by a certain lion-hunter one day as he lay under a tree in a garden; a little speech, obviously prepared beforehand, was delivered, in which was duly set forth the speaker's enormous admiration for the composer's works and his overpowering sense of honour he felt at the interview—in fact the whole stock-in-trade of the professional "interviewer" was employed, just a little too evidently. The temptation to punish the stranger, whom we may fancy to have been a person of a full habit, was too much for Brahms, who interrupted the flow of enthusiasm with the remark, "Stop, my dear sir, there must be some mistake here. I have no doubt you are looking for my brother, the composer; I'm sorry to say he has just gone out for a walk, but if you make haste and run along that path, through the wood, and up yonder hill, you may probably still catch him up."

He is seen at his best in the small circle of his intimate friends, among whom he enjoys the reputation not only of being witty, full of fun, and, in the best sense, "good company," but of possessing a kind heart and a most generous disposition. His Spartan simplicity of life is one of the many points of resemblance with Beethoven, which extend to such physical characteristics as the thickset build, small stature, and the proportion, or want of proportion, between the body and the lionlike head, with its eyes "of penetrating regard and fire and nobility of expression." Unlike the generality of musicians, he is a great reader, and his conversation, even on matters unconnected with his art, is that of a highly cultivated intellect. A less unusual peculiarity is the intense interest which a new work of his own excites in him, as long as it is in progress, or, in fact, until it is first performed; this ordeal past, it seems to be laid aside, as far as the composer's memory is concerned, and nothing is harder, even for his intimates, than to get him to talk about his past compositions. For the opinion of outsiders on his work he has the profoundest contempt, and is completely indifferent to journalistic verdicts. His almost filial devotion to Madame Schumann is a graceful trait in his character.

It is no doubt mainly the dread of being made a lion of that has kept him away from England, where he has so many admirers and unknown friends. On two occasions he has been offered the degree of Doctor of Music by the University of Cambridge, but both times has declined to come to receive it. The chief loss occasioned by his refusal, from an artistic point of view, is that English audiences have not heard him conduct one of his orchestral compositions; these, however, have been so constantly kept in the programmes of the

Richter and other concerts, and so admirably interpreted, that the loss is greatly lessened. There is, after all, no possible reason why a man may not decline a proffered distinction that involves a somewhat formidable journey to receive it, and we may conclude that Brahms knows his own interests as well as we can know them. He is rich enough in distinctions of all kinds, one of the most important being the degree of Doctor of Philosophy granted by the University of Breslau.

Up to the time at which he went to live in Vienna purely orchestral music had occupied a secondary place in his sphere of work, and it is not without reason that his career in this direction is generally considered to have begun with the first of his symphonies, which dates from 1875. Shortly before this was written, some further contributions to instrumental chamber-music were made, the numbers of which in the catalogue come close to those of the choral compositions lately spoken of. These, the three string quartets, opp. 51 and 67, and a third quartet for piano and strings, op. 60 in C minor, undoubtedly show certain signs of labour; they "smell of the lamp" a little, and seem to indicate that in this particular direction the vein was for the time exhausted; this is all the more remarkable since the choral works dating from the same period, the "Liebeslieder" (both sets), and many of the numerous songs of the time, are among the most widely accepted and most genial of his earlier compositions. Perhaps, as far as chamber-music was concerned, it was a case of *reculer pour mieux sauter*, since he was within measurable distance of a work which was received as the first of a new series of masterpieces in this department, the first of the violin sonatas.

The first symphony, which still remains to be spoken of, has a special interest to English amateurs, since it was the work by which the composer was represented among others who actually took the Cambridge degree at the time when it was first offered to Brahms. A curious coincidence marks it in connection with the performance at Cambridge, and accounts for the practice into which amateurs have fallen of calling it the "Cambridge Symphony." In the impressive introduction to the final Allegro, the subject of which, by the way, is a curiously faithful pendant to (by no means a replica of) the theme of the finale of Beethoven's Choral

Symphony, the horn has a short phrase which would arrest attention anywhere, but which, in Cambridge, struck a most familiar note; for it is identical in its first two sections with certain of the chimes known as the "Cambridge quarters"—that pretty set of four-note phrases said to have been arranged by Crotch from a passage in "I know that my Redeemer liveth," which has gradually spread from St. Mary's Church till it has become the best-known arrangement for marking the quarters of the hour. Of course the composer did not know this, nor, indeed, was the symphony written for the occasion at which it was performed at the English University; it had been heard at Carlsruhe in November 1876, while the Cambridge celebration, at which it was conducted by Joachim, did not take place until the following March.

Four sets of songs only separate this impressive and important work in Brahms' catalogue from his second symphony in D major, op. 73, a work in strongest contrast to the first. Many passages in the C minor symphony remain difficult to grasp, even after a second or even a third hearing; in the three first movements this is particularly the case, and it would be useless to deny that the work as a whole is by no means one of the most generally pleasing of the master's compositions. In the new symphony a delicious and almost pastoral quietude prevails; the subjects are even "taking" in their simple beauty, recalling sometimes one or other of the waltzes of Schubert or of the minuets of Mozart. There is a bewitching passage in the *allegretto grazioso*, which reminds one of a child pretending to be completely transformed, and firmly believing that it is unrecognisable, when it has tied a handkerchief under its chin and pulled a grimace. The little theme of the minuet-like opening suddenly appears in two-four time, with all the airs of being new, but really unaltered in any important particular, and the effect of the device is most charming. Both subjects of the lovely finale deserve to rank with the most beautiful inventions in music, and their treatment is no less masterly than their conception is felicitous. The Haydnesque character of the movement may point back to the beautiful variations on that master's "Chorale Sancti Antonii" (Brahms' op. 56) which were among his most important works of preparation for his first symphony. Two works of the greatest value and importance to violinists are among the compositions which occupy an intermediate place between the second and third symphonies; these are: op. 77, the violin concerto, written for Joachim, and often played by him in England, and the first sonata for violin and piano in G, op. 78. The former, in the same key as the single concerto of Beethoven's for the instrument, is, of all modern concertos, the one most worthy to stand beside it; the same subjection of individual display to general effect—using that word in its highest sense—distinguish both, and the serene beauty of themes is as conspicuous in the later work as in the earlier. As show-pieces, neither is likely to oust Mendelssohn's concerto and those of other popular writers in the affections of the multitude of fiddlers; but the violinists who are also artists in the true sense will come to recognise the real opportunities for making a deep impression—not merely of provoking applause—that are contained in Brahms' as in Beethoven's work. As an example of the perfect friendship and unity of artistic conviction existing between the composer and the great artist for whom he wrote, it may be mentioned that Joachim contributed the cadenzas to his friend's composition, passages in which no lack of continuity or homogeneity can be traced by the keenest critic. For Joachim, too, there can be no doubt that the last movement, with its distinctively Hungarian colouring, was especially designed, and we may be sure that it will be a very long time before another artist arises to play it as he does. The exquisite subject of the slow movement, with its lovely touches of orchestral effect, is an example of the composer's invention at its greatest height, and it would be difficult to match it, or indeed the movement as a whole, for melodious beauty.

The second of the two violin compositions, the sonata in G, has throughout a singularly winning character, and it is certain that none of the works of his later life has gained him more admirers, from those who formerly stood aloof. A wonderful degree of unity in expression prevails from the beginning of the first *vivace ma non troppo* to the quiet close of the sonata in which a "plagal cadence" is employed with the happiest effect. The beautiful *adagio* flows on its even course, and is brought in again in the finale, as if to calm down the slight restlessness of the main subject of this movement. To this main subject attaches a peculiar interest, for it is one of the rare instances in which a modern master has successfully adopted the device which Handel was wont to employ in order to save himself the trouble of inventing new music. We may be quite sure that this was not the motive by which Brahms was impelled when he took the theme of a song written some years before for the finale of his sonata. In the album of songs, op. 59, is one called "Regenlied," in which the figure of accompaniment gives exactly the dreary effect of pattering rain, while the plaintive vocal theme carries out the impression of a gentle inquietude. It is quite a different kind of weather from that reflected in a celebrated prelude of Chopin's suggested by a prolonged storm in Corsica; but if less tragic than that in its emotion, the song is not less expressive or artistic. In Chopin's prelude you are made to feel with the composer the hopelessness with which a child regards something it sees no end to; in Brahms' song we know the rain will stop, and that the restless feeling excited by it is only a passing mood. The composer was evidently taken with the subject and its figure of accompaniment, for the next song in the series to which "Regenlied" belongs, called "Nachklang," carries on both, though to a different purpose. In the finale of the sonata both appear again, but the figure of accompaniment is no longer confined to one part, as it had to be in the songs; its possibilities are now more fully taken advantage of, and it is surprising, to those who knew the songs first, to see the process by which their material has been utilised for instrumental purposes. No work of the master's has met with wider acceptance than this, which displayed his powers in a direction hitherto untried, unless we may include the violoncello sonata in E minor, as belonging to the same group—a place it hardly deserves, since with all the beauty of its opening movement, and the winsome charm of its minuet, the somewhat crabbed character of its canonic finale marks it as belonging to the composer's less genial days.

Immediately before and after the two violin pieces just mentioned were two sets of pianoforte solos, op. 76, a set of eight so-called "Capriccios and Intermezzi," and op. 79, two Rhapsodies. It has never been Brahms' habit to seek out effective titles for his smaller works, such as were beloved of Schumann; for this reason, perhaps, they have been less popular with the typical amateur than those of the older master. Still, without going into "fancy" descriptions, some more suitable names might have been found for both sets of pieces. A few of the "capriccios" have, indeed, the fantastic, unruly wilfulness implied in the title, and, besides being very difficult to play, are certainly interesting, and in a sense beautiful, notably one in B minor involving a perfect command of the staccato. But intermezzos that are apparently intended to take no intermediary place, but to stand as independent pieces, seem a little wrongly named, and certainly anything less rhapsodical than the two regularly-constructed pieces in almost conventional "da capo" form to which the name of rhapsody is applied can hardly be imagined. But, titles apart, both sets have manifold beauties and points of interest; the intermezzo in A flat is the most suitably written for the pianoforte of the earlier set, but both the rhapsodies appeal to pianists as much as to the lover of music. It is not one of Brahms' merits, any more than it was one of Beethoven's, to write what is called "grateful" music for the pianoforte alone; few of his pieces of any period "play themselves" as do those of Mendelssohn in one school, those of Chopin in another, or those of Liszt in a third. The peculiar and distinctive qualities of the instrument have not, apparently, found in him a very loving interpreter, and only here and there, and then mainly in concerted music, does the pianist find his work congenial from the technical point of view. Like all great originators, he has invented passages which require a special technique for themselves, and the handfuls of chords, the sudden extensions, and the rapid changes of position, in which he freely indulges, have to be carefully studied; there are formidable difficulties enough, in all conscience, in the writers I have named, yet they undoubtedly yield a more satisfactory result to the student than do the works of Brahms. It must be understood that the quality here spoken of is one that affects none but players. It is entirely independent of musical merit, and, as has been well said, music that is easy to play is not always easy to listen to. To put ease of vocal or instrumental effect in a high place among the virtues of a composer is surely to see things in their wrong proportion. Both the rhapsodies, particularly the one in G minor, are genuine "pianoforte music" in the sense that is so rare with Brahms, and the two pieces are most deservedly popular with the better class of players.

Next to them came out two overtures, of course

for full orchestra: **op. 80,** "Akademische **Fest-Ouvertüre**," and op. 81, "Tragische Ouvertüre": the former, written in recognition of the degree **of** doctor of philosophy conferred upon the **composer** by the University of Breslau, was privately performed in that place on January 4, 1881; and both were soon afterwards played at Vienna, **and very** coldly received. The first is built for **the most part upon the** themes of German **students'** songs, **such** as are **familiar** to every German audience: many, like the "Gaudeamus," with which the work closes most brilliantly, **are** scarcely less well known in England. **Still,** though it is justly popular among us, its success in its native country has been, and certainly will be, far greater. One of the most humorous passages in the work has been discounted for English audiences by the familiarity of a certain device employed in it—a device which has not yet been done to death in Germany, as it has with us. After a pause, the bassoon enters with intensely comic effect, with the theme of what is known as the "Fuchslied" or freshmen's song ("Was kommt dort von der Höh'?"); the point of the joke, the quality of **tone of the** instrument chosen, falls a little flat with English audiences, as, since its first appearance in the

Sorcerer's song, the bassoon jest has been drawn upon for a safe laugh in any comic opera when the wit of the dialogue has run a little thin. The "Tragic" overture wants no "programme" for its elucidation; what may be the particular form of fate that so obviously hangs over it until the trombones bring about the final catastrophe we are not told, but the course of the story is plain enough to those who have ears to hear, and most impressive it is.

The two choral works which precede the third symphony, and which are the last compositions for choir and orchestra that the master has given us, again deal with the problem of human destiny. The first, "Nänie," set to Schiller's words, was suggested by the death of the promising young painter, Feuerbach, a great friend of the composer's, and it is dedicated to the mother of the artist. It has suffered, in England especially, from a comparison with Goetz's setting of the same words, which occupied the attention of amateurs just about the time when Brahms' setting came out. The romantic circumstances of Goetz's early death, and the vogue which his posthumous works enjoyed for a brief season in England, were enough to account for this preference, and, beside this, there is much to be said for the earlier composition, which is one of its author's most happily inspired creations, while Brahms' version is not by any means the best of his works in this form. On the strength of this verdict of the musical world, a certain set of critics tried to persuade themselves that the dead composer was in every way greater than the living, and quite recently one of the chiefs of the "irresponsible" school of writers has repeated the assertion. It is a thankless task to play Devil's Advocate with a posthumous fame, but it has come to be very generally recognised as possible that Goetz did not die so very prematurely, and that in fact some of his later works betrayed certain mannerisms which threatened to become more noticeable as time went on. In regard to his actual achievement, beautiful as much of his work undoubtedly is, and high as is its general level, it were absurd to set it up against the whole body of Brahms' work, which, although it has left opera untouched, has covered every other branch of art, and with absolute success in all. In the other choral work of this time, the "Gesang der Parzen," from Goethe's *Iphigenia*, a six-part chorus is employed, and some impressive antiphonal effects are thus made possible; in feeling, it is a curious counterpart and contrast to the "Schicksalslied," though it is scarcely as fine. The second pianoforte concerto, in B flat, op. 83, is not wholly free from the tragic intensity of these two works, in spite of its strikingly beautiful opening, in which the announcement of the theme is given to the horn; it abounds in formidable difficulties in the solo part, and can hardly be ranked among the most attractive of the composer's works, at least to any but diligent students, who will find much to interest them in its construction. A somewhat forbidding trio for piano and strings, op. 87, and a very interesting string quintet, op. 88, complete the number of instrumental works that preceded the third symphony; but some three books of songs are of the same date, and it is very curious to find, just in one of the less genial periods of the master's activity, such a delightfully humorous song as "Vergebliches Ständchen" or the suave melody of "Feldeinsamkeit"—songs which rank with the best, as well as the most popular, of the composer's vocal works.

As with the first pair of symphonies, so with the second: nothing but vocal works of comparatively small calibre separate them in the list of works, although no less than two years elapsed between the publication of the third and fourth, which appeared respectively in 1883 and 1885. The third, op. 90, in F major, is as easy to follow as the symphony in D, while its themes have even greater value and individuality. Each as it comes strikes us as a new revelation of beauty, and the well-devised contrast, not only between the successive subjects themselves, but between the movements constructed on them, makes for their appreciation. For example, the first theme of the opening movement, given out by the violins, sweeps along through a compass of nearly two octaves, with an altogether irresistible *élan ;* the second subject moves by small intervals and has a range of six notes, its smoothness of phrasing being again in contrast to the dashing, broken rhythms of its companion. The lovely andante proceeds from a tune of almost religious character; to the younger generation of musicians it loses nothing by an accidental resemblance which is apt to bother older hearers, for its first group of notes is unmistakably like the once famous prayer in "Zampa," and although, as it is hardly necessary to say, Brahms' way of treating it considerably differs from Hérold's, the similarity remains. It is difficult to think of anything in its way more perfect than the *poco allegretto* which occupies the place of the scherzo, and which has all the plaintive grace of Schubert at his very best. The finale has been not inaptly likened to a battle; the determination of the opening subject, in F minor, and the wild outcries of the violins later on, would of themselves suggest this, even without the presence of a most realistic passage for the violoncellos, which is as joyous a shout of victory as ever was uttered.

The fourth symphony, in E minor, op. 98, is far less attractive to the casual hearer than its predecessor, and now and then a return is made for a short time to the crabbed manner of some of the earlier works. The same contrast as that noticed in the F major symphony, between a theme of wide range and one of closer texture, occurs here; but neither subject has anything like the amount of actual beauty possessed by its counterpart, though the dramatic character of the movement, and the masterly treatment to which the themes and their subsidiaries are subjected, give it interest and value of another kind. The andante, built on an extremely simple and balladlike melody, is certainly the most taking of the four sections, for the *presto*, with its somewhat archaic flavour, is not of surpassing interest. The finale is the movement in virtue of which the symphony may claim a place of its own among the landmarks of instrumental music. A survey of all the typical symphonies since the form first had its rise, would make it quite clear that each of the three first movements has, in the course of years, attained to what may be called an ideal form. The "sonata form" for the first movement; the "extended lied-form," or "aria form," for the slow movement; and the "*da capo* form," in more or less developed guise, for the scherzo, minuet, intermezzo, or whatever the section may be called—have evidently satisfied the great masters of the symphony, and exceptions to the types are neither numerous nor successful. With the finale it is different; the rondo form, once accepted almost universally, has not, in the later and greater days of the symphony, fulfilled the requirements of composers, and it is interesting to see how in this section, more than in any other, experiments have been made. Take Beethoven's nine masterpieces, and you will find the old type of rondo occurring in only three at most; in one a set of variations, in others a free adaptation of the "sonata form" replaces it, and the splendid formlessness of the finale of the Choral Symphony is, perhaps, the strongest proof of all that accepted types were insufficient, the more so since in the other sections of this very symphony the traditional forms are preserved, not, indeed, without modification, but with no change of any essential feature. There was, therefore, every excuse for making innovations in this movement, since no type hitherto invented had been found perfect; and in applying to it a form already in existence, though for some time obsolete in connexion with compositions of large calibre, the modern composer showed his wisdom. It is not necessary to enter into the subtle distinction between the English "ground" or "ground bass," the French "chaconne," and the Italian "passacaglia"; it is enough to say that certain features common to them all, and some peculiar to one or other of the two last, are employed by Brahms in this place, and that the form which had been virtually dormant ever since Bach's time has received a new lease of life from the modern composer. The immediate suggestion must have come from that monumental chaconne of Bach for violin alone which Joachim has made so familiar, and of which Brahms wrote a pianoforte arrangement. Bach's wonderful succession of variations on a constantly recurring theme of eight bars, changes its course suddenly in the middle, and it is easy for a not very attentive listener to lose the connecting thread of the music, and to think that the phrase is absent when it is overlaid with ornament or represented by its essential sequence of harmonies. In like manner in the symphony, even those who keep their attention fixed on the phrase in their analytical programmes, find themselves, after a time, foiled in the effort to trace it; and, losing this, they lose all, for the interest of the variations as they pass is not likely to impress itself on hearers who are busy searching for a series of notes they cannot hear. In truth, this movement cannot as yet be completely grasped or enjoyed except by those who not only follow the score, but have studied it to some extent beforehand, and it is no wonder that many who have not taken the trouble to do this should find the work nothing but a rather tiresome riddle. Their position is an exact parallel to that of amateurs not so very long ago, who voted the Ninth Symphony an unintelligible piece of work, showing a sad falling off in a composer whose earlier works had won their admiration—if indeed they did not look upon it as the incoherent ravings of a lunatic who also chanced to be deaf. To show how easily the thread of this finale may be lost, or rather never found, it may be mentioned that the analysis of it given in Hermann Kretzschmar's useful "Führer durch den Concertsaal" contains no mention of the phrase out of which the whole movement is developed.

Three new examples of chamber-music were the next product of the composer's genius, and in these it was clear that he had perfectly regained, not only his power—that, in fact, he had never lost—but his geniality of utterance in this branch of music. Perhaps the least valuable of the three is the violoncello sonata in F, op. 99, the beautiful slow movement of which shows a decided, though possibly not wholly successful, innovation in the matter of key-relationship, being laid out in the key of F sharp major. The strange effect of the "leading-note" of the new movement being identical with the keynote of that which has gone before is a little perplexing to the hearer, and its excuse is that the theme of the second movement seems to require a feeling of ambiguous tonality. The device, though no doubt the composer adopted it, as he does all, most logically, can hardly be held up for imitation. Op. 100, a second sonata for piano and violin, is a fitting companion to the lovely sonata in G; it opens, in A major, with a theme that is oddly like that of the "Preislied" in "Die Meistersinger," but of a far quieter and less impassioned character. The second movement is another of those experiments of which the composer gave us so many just at this point; it combines a slow movement of very beautiful expression, in F major, with a scherzo in D minor, both appearing alternately, until the rapid section, which has increased in vivacity with each repetition, finishes off with what may be called a whisk of its tail. The mysterious pianoforte arpeggios which are so prominent a feature of the finale reappear, but with quite a different effect, in the trio, op. 101, for piano and strings, in a dainty little presto of that half-playful, half-plaintive kind of which there are many examples, particularly in Brahms' later compositions. The slow movement is in "seven-four" time, the same rhythm as the Hungarian song on which the composer wrote an early set of variations. The test of such departures from the usual rhythmic forms is that the thing should sound perfectly natural when it is done; for instance, the beautiful little piece in F major, the second of Schumann's "Stücke in Volkston," never seems to depart from perfect symmetry and grace of movement, and yet its rhythm of seven bars is one of its chief characteristics. Here, too, the natural, easy swing of a popular melody is perfectly preserved, though the theme has far more of what the Germans call "import" than any traditional tune known to collectors.

It has often seemed as though Brahms fell in love with one particular instrument or group of instruments at one particular time, and this batch of chamber compositions was so far from exhausting his interest, even temporarily, in the violin and violoncello, that it was immediately succeeded by a concerto for the two instruments with orchestra, another revival of old established but long neglected usage; for the concerto in which one solo instrument takes part is of less ancient date than that in which several occupy the prominent position. To entrust the solo part, as we should call it now, to a number of instruments, called in old days the "concertino," was, of course, to do away with many of those opportunities for individual display which are supposed to be, and with performers perhaps are, among the chief attractions of the concerto form; and it may well be imagined that this of itself would commend the older variety to a composer who has nearly as strong an objection as Schumann had to effect for effect's sake. Written for Joachim, and the most distinguished artist among the members of his famous quartet, Herr Robert Hausmann, the work contains difficulties of every kind, though these are not its most striking characteristic. Perhaps the first thing that arrests attention in the concerto is its continual variety of tone-colour, and the curious results obtained by the combination of the solo instruments either alone or with the orchestra. In an important passage the two stringed instruments, each playing double notes, are made to sound like a string quartet, and the cadenza of the first movement is a marvel of ingenuity. The exquisite melody of the slow movement, given out by both soloists, is not insisted on as it would have been in the hands of a less original writer; and as a consequence it makes less impression

JOHANNES BRAHMS

upon a general audience than it deserves to do.

The next work published was in some sort a combination of two of the forms in which Brahms had most successfully caught the popular ear; the "Zigeunerlieder," as his op. 103 is called, are a number of short compositions based on themes of distinctively Hungarian or Gipsy character (the two are so much alike that it takes an expert to differentiate them), in which much of the charm and "go" of the Hungarian dances is found again; they are set for four voices with piano accompaniment, and in the handling of the vocal parts we are often reminded of the "Liebeslieder." The piano (solo) accompaniment occasionally imitates the characteristic effects of the "cimbalom," but to a far less realistic extent than is done, for example, in Mr. Korbay's clever arrangements of Hungarian songs. Three more sets of single songs, and then came the third of the sonatas for piano and violin, the beautiful work in D minor, op. 108, which at once became as popular as either of its predecessors. It appealed by its originality and charm to intelligent amateurs, and by the masterly treatment of its first movement to lovers of structural peculiarities, for in both sections of the movement a long "pedal point" occurs, and the extraordinary freedom of the composer's gait in what would have been merely fetters to less accomplished men cannot fail to provoke astonishment and admiration. The deep expression of the slow movement, the fairylike grace and the stormy vigour of the finale, though none of them reveal any new characteristic in the master, are elements which have endeared the sonata to large numbers of musicians, whether players or listeners. A set of three short motets for eight-part choir *a capella*, entitled "Fest- und Gedenksprüche," written in celebration of three important national events (the battle of Leipzig, 1813; that of Sedan, 1871; and the unification of the German Empire), were first heard at an industrial exhibition at Hamburg, in September 1889; all three are masterly in construction and impressive in the highest degree. These, together with a book of three motets, op. 110, preceded a very beautiful string quintet with an unusually prominent part for the first viola, op. 111. The set of canons, op. 113, ends with one that illustrates an odd peculiarity of the composer's, a certain carelessness in giving titles to his works and in acknowledging their sources when they are built upon borrowed material. This sounds a little like the Handelian method of "conveying" other people's ideas and using them in works of his own without either asking leave or acknowledging indebtedness; but in the case of the living composer, he has borrowed, where he has borrowed, from quarters so well known to all musicians, that if there were any intention of palming off the themes as his own, conviction must have followed on the instant. The tunes used by Brahms in his "Hungarian Dances" were familiar as household words to all who knew the music of the country, or indeed to those who were only conversant with the "czardas" through Liszt's Rhapsodies; still, some misunderstandings arose from no mention being made on the title-page that they were not original melodies by Brahms, and some sapient person wrote to an English musical paper giving the names of other composers for whom their invention was claimed, and no doubt thinking himself as skilful a musical detective as the first discoverer of the various compositions appropriated in "Israel in Egypt." In like manner, some note referring to the songs

"Regenlied" and "Nachklang" would undoubtedly have given additional interest to the finale of Brahms' first violin sonata; and the last of the canons just mentioned would have lost nothing if it had pleased the composer to call it a vocal transcription of Schubert's plaintive song "Der Leyermann," for such, with very slight alteration—made necessary in order to bring it into canonic shape—it is. An earlier instance occurs in a set of 15 "Volkskinderlieder," some lovely arrangements of traditional tunes, published without acknowledgment of their source, and indeed without Brahms' name. They were dedicated to the children of Robert and Clara Schumann, and no doubt are among the first-fruits of the composer's genius. The dear little lullaby "Sandmännchen" is scarcely less popular than the lovely and original cradle-song, "Guten Abend, gut' Nacht," from op. 49. The six vocal quartets, op. 112, which followed the string quintet, were in part a kind of aftermath of the "Zigeunerlieder"; they include four more quartets which seem to belong to the former set, beside two very beautiful compositions in strong contrast with these, suave and flowing broadly, and powerfully imagined.

JOHANNES BRAHMS

It has often been noticed that Brahms' compositions have come out in pairs, and the foregoing analysis of the catalogue of his works has given many instances of the kind; there are yet four more before the end is reached. Whether the discovery of an exceptionally gifted clarinet-player inspired the composer, as Weber's admiration for the greatest clarinettist of his day gave rise to some of his most charming compositions, cannot be definitely stated, but any amateur who heard Herr Mühlfeld play the two new works of Brahms which appeared in 1892 will have no difficulty in believing this to have been the case. It is probably an accident that led to the trio for pianoforte, violin and clarinet being numbered op. 114, while its companion, the quintet for clarinet and strings, appeared as op. 115; but whether this be the case or not, it cannot be denied that the master kept the best till the last. It was wise, too, to let English audiences become acquainted with the quintet, and with the powers of the artist for whose special use it was written, before introducing the other work to the patrons of the Popular Concerts. Of course, by this means, the quintet carried off all the honour, and perhaps the trio came in for rather too much abuse; still, the feeling of disappointment which it created after the wonderful and immediate success of its companion was not to be dissimulated. It is in truth one of the works in which the intellect of the composer rather than his heart seems to have been engaged; the theme of the *andantino grazioso* which stands in the place of a scherzo is considerably below the master's usual level of refinement, and the pleasantest impression left by the work is of the graceful and characteristic second subject of the first movement.

The quintet may or may not have been designed with a definite purpose of showing off Herr Mühlfeld's extraordinary powers; if it were it succeeded beyond all anticipation, and the impression the work and the player made upon the conservative "Pop" audience was a thing to remember. The artist's wonderful command of his breath enabled him to deliver the leading theme of the first movement with a smoothness quite unexpected by those who were most familiar with the difficulties of the instrument, and the not unnatural feeling of resentment at the importation of a foreign player—which, by the way, involved the temporary adoption of a reasonable pitch, a rare thing at an English concert—gave way at once to whole-hearted admiration. The theme in question contains what has been called in the works of Wagner an "essential turn," that is to say, a group of notes in form identical with a turn, but being an organic part of the theme, not a mere fortuitous accretion. Such a group of notes, common enough with Wagner, is most rare with Brahms, and it is indeed difficult to call to mind another instance of it in his works. Every one of the six notes of which this turn consists was phrased with an exquisite sense of proportion which few players, except Joachim, ever exhibit, and which appears to lie entirely outside the ken of singers. In such a passage as that with which the wonderful slow movement closes, and in which a long phrase of melodious beauty is given out first by the clarinet and then by the first violin, it seemed inevitable, according to all former experience, that a deeper meaning, a warmer expression, and a nobler emotion, should be put into it on its repetition by the leader—at least, when Joachim occupied that position—than at its first occurrence; but so complete was the clarinettist's artistic endowment that nothing was left for the violinist to improve upon. The freedom, too, with which the dramatic ornamentations of the same movement (which are strongly tinged with Hungarian colouring) were executed, left no room for question as to the composer's wisdom in insisting on Herr Mühlfeld's engagement at the London concerts, and the public appreciation of the artist and the work with which his name will be inseparably connected, in England at least, must have made the managerial speculation well worth while, even from a lower standpoint than the purely artistic.

The groups of pianoforte solos which make up the latest publications of Brahms, leave, like their predecessors, the so-called "rhapsodies," etc., something to be desired in the way of nomenclature and even arrangement. Op. 116, called collectively "Fantasien," consists of eight pieces, named either intermezzo or capriccio according as their pace is slow or fast, and their character sedate or restless. In key-relationship, style, and other qualities, few of these are disposed in what seems to be the best order for performance in public; indeed, this order does not seem to have been yet discovered, since each pianist who has essayed them in London has made a different selection and has played them in a different sequence. The powerful capriccio in G minor, with its beautiful melody in E flat, resembling in character the youthful fire and richly harmonious style of the early piano sonatas; the romantic intermezzo in E major, with its graceful effects of crossed hands—a real piece of "pianoforte music" in the strictest sense; the charming minuet in the same key; and the fine capriccio in D minor, in which a bravura passage, that rarest thing with Brahms, occupies a prominent place, are the most valuable of the set, which, as a whole, cannot compare with its companion series of three intermezzi, op. 117. Of these, the first, on an entrancingly beautiful subject, a little like the English carol, "The First Nowell," is the most sure of immediate popularity; its motto from Herder's "Volkslieder"—

"*Schlaf sanft, mein Kind, schlaf sanft und schön,
Mich dauert's sehr, dich weinen sehn,*"

is ostensibly of Scottish origin, though it is difficult to identify; at all events it gives the suggestion of a lullaby, and as such the piece is a worthy pendant to the simple song lately mentioned, though its middle section breathes of weightier issues than the words seem to authorise. The second piece, a rather Schumannesque composition in B flat minor, is elegant and, in the hands of a competent player, effective, with its airy passages of tender melody; and the third, a ballad-like piece of longer extent than any of the other intermezzi, founded on a subject resembling that of the finale of the composer's third symphony, is remarkable for the exquisite grace with which the return to the first theme is made. Another set of "Clavierstücke" appeared at the end of last year. Op. 118 contains six pieces (four intermezzi, a ballade, and a romance); the ballade, in G minor, is as vigorous as anything the master has given us, and the romance, with its rhythmic changes and its exquisite middle section in a pastoral mood, is a real inspiration; the last intermezzo, too, is most poetical. Op. 119 consists of three more intermezzi, one in E minor, of enchanting beauty in the "alternative" section and another, in C, a delicious little scherzo; to wind up the whole set, there is a "rhapsodie" of formidable difficulty and great beauty, constructed on a theme of five-bar rhythm. A book of fifty-one Uebungen appeared almost at the same time; although these are studies of a purely technical kind, in one and all musical interest as well as practical value is to be found. A new set of songs is spoken of, and faint rumours are heard of a "Faust" overture as shortly to be brought out.

I have left the multitude of Brahms' songs to be spoken of together, since they are even less divisible into distinct periods than any of his instrumental works. The dramatic note struck in the first of them all, the beautiful "Liebestreu" ("O versenk") recurs again and again throughout the long series, and these, together with the romantic atmosphere he, like other great song-writers of Germany, has succeeded so often in obtaining, are the strongest characteristics they exhibit. In actual dramatic utterance, though examples are not so many as of the more lyrical kind, there are quite enough to prove that the composer could deal with a strongly dramatic situation as powerfully and truly as with any other. In the picturesque "Von ewiger Liebe," and many other songs and duets, in which two persons are supposed to take part, such as the humorous "Vergebliches Ständchen" and the rest, the characters are "individualised" as strongly within the limits of a single song as they could be in a whole opera. But, at the same time, his lyrics are the best production of his muse in the direction of vocal music. To enumerate the songs of lasting beauty he has given us in this branch would take far too long, but mention must be made of such perfect works as "Ruhe, Süssliebchen," and many another of the "Magelonelieder," "Wehe, Lüftchen," "O komme, holde Sommernacht"—a song strangely neglected by the small number of vocalists who can do justice to the master's music—the duet "Phänomen," the justly popular "Meine Liebe ist grün," the exquisitely melodious and deeply felt "Minnelied," "Sapphische Ode," and "Wie Melodien." These date from widely different portions of Brahms' life, but all have the mark of the same genius. Such splendid outbursts of manly vigour as "O Lady Judith" and the intensely powerful "Verrath" are, however, found only among the later books of his songs. Those who have penetrated most deeply into the spirit of the composer's lyrics would make, it may be, a different list if they were asked to name their favourites; but these are works which must win acceptance from every cultivated musician. In what may be called musical landscape-painting, there are a number of instances to prove him to be a most accomplished master of a branch of art that he has not specially cultivated in the deliberate way in which some other composers have set themselves to achieve fame. "Mainacht" is a perfect specimen of this, and all the more so that the portrayal of a night in early summer with nightingales' song and lovers' vows is one of the commonplaces of the hack song-writer. "Verzagen" gives us the very sound of the sea, with waves restlessly drawing back from a stony beach and reflecting the mental tension of some modern Ariadne on the shore; and in "Feldeinsamkeit," a picture of a summer day with little clouds drifting lazily through the blue heaven, is given as faithfully as though the medium were colour, instead of sound. A more suggestive or picturesque barcarolle than "Auf dem See" can hardly be imagined, although the recognised figure of accompaniment for such pieces is unused. Some of the most purely lyrical of the composer's vocal works are to be found among the unaccompanied choral compositions, such as the six "Lieder und Romanzen," op. 93*a*, or the five-part songs, op. 104. The second of the former set, "Stand das Mädchen," a quaint and most characteristic little song, appears in op. 95 as a solo with accompaniment, here as a part-song with a soprano solo *obbligato*.

The tender "Fahr wohl, o Vöglein!" with its beautiful effect of *diminuendo*, is an absolutely perfect little piece of writing in this popular form and is as easily intelligible as the most hackneyed of Mendelssohn's part-songs for open-air performance. The later set contains things far more deeply felt and more beautifully expressed than the earlier. The two first, both called "Nachtwache," are among the master's most individual creations; and the second, with its antiphonal effects, imitating the answering horn-notes of the watchmen—"Ruhn Sie?—Sie ruhn"—is a wonderful instance of vivid suggestion of orchestral colouring by the human voice alone. All these five are most beautiful, and all are in the same sombre mood.

Among the small group of works not included in the numbered catalogue of Brahms' compositions, the best known are the Hungarian dances, originally published as a pianoforte duet, in two books, subsequently arranged by the composer for orchestra and by Joachim for violin and piano, and finally completed by the addition, not very many years since, of two more books. The charming set of "15 Volkskinderlieder," dedicated to the Schumann children, has been already referred to; there remain to be mentioned a chorale prelude and fugue for the organ on the theme of " O Traurigkeit, o Herzeleid ! " a fugue in A flat minor for the same instrument, a setting of the song " Mondnacht " (not improbably excluded from the numbered list out of reverence for Schumann's well-known setting of the same words), and a group of arrangements for the piano some of which exhibit him in an almost mischievous mood. The beautiful F minor study from the second book of Chopin's immortal twenty-four, is transformed into an exercise of really hideous difficulty by the change of the right-hand part from single notes to sixths; the " moto perpetuo " from Weber's sonatas in C major is, in like manner, turned upside down, the part for the two hands being interchanged, and other alterations made; and the famous violin chaconne of Bach is transcribed for the left hand alone. This, and the two arrangements of the same master's presto from the sonata in G minor for violin alone, have a far higher value than the transcriptions just mentioned, and the concert-version of Gluck's well-known gavotte in A from " Paride ed Elena " (a version made for the use of Mme. Schumann) treats the charming piece with complete reverence. One most interesting composition has remained in manuscript for many years: the movement contributed to a sonata for violin and piano, composed as a gift of welcome to Joachim by Schumann, Albert Dietrich, and Brahms, on the occasion of the illustrious violinist's visit to Düsseldorf in 1853. It would be most interesting to see the work in which two of the greatest German masters collaborated, and it is to be hoped that the fortunate artist in whose honour it was written will some day introduce it to English audiences.

Two sonatas for violin and piano by C. P. E. Bach, recently re-issued, are said to have been furnished by Brahms with amplifications of the figured bass of the original; the self-restraint with which this has been done, and the entire simplicity of the filling-up, are marks of the true artist's hand, and the study of these beautiful pieces may be recommended, not only to violinists—who would find them a very effective and valuable addition to their repertory—but to those who undertake to make accompaniments to the old masterpieces of chamber-music, and who are too often tempted to show off their own ingenuity at the composer's expense. Another work of the same kind is the accompaniment to an edition of Handel's vocal duets.

JOHANNES BRAHMS

The reprint of Couperin's "Suites de Pièces," edited by Brahms and Dr. Chrysander, contains nothing but the original text; and the composer's editorial work on the committees formed for the issues of the complete works of Bach, Mozart, and Chopin, brought out by the firm of Breitkopf und Härtel, is, of course, only critical.

In other ways than these, and apart from his musical compositions, Brahms has not been without influence on the art of his time, since we owe to him the "discovery" of Dvorák, whose early compositions, represented only by the album of vocal duets, "Moravské dvojpăvy," struck him as possessing real originality and power, and as giving brilliant promise for the future. If we consider the subsequent works of the Bohemian composer, we shall be apt to wonder at the exceptionally favourable opinion formed of his powers by a composer whose chief characteristic is the masterly manipulation of the established forms of music. But Dvorák's lack of skill in dealing with these, his inability to subject his material to interesting development, and the constructive weakness exhibited in his more ambitious works, had not then declared themselves, and his freshness of invention and unconventional way of expressing himself no doubt appealed strongly to Brahms, whose hatred of anything like "capellmeistermusik" is as great as Wagner's. The German master has not always been so tolerant of the work even of his best contemporaries, and there are many stories, told on good authority, of the chilling silence or the crushing remarks with which he has received the compositions of certain composers, and these not by any means the least distinguished among living musicians. One of these played through to Brahms the score of a work since accepted with favour by the best German critics, and received, for all criticism on his music, the remark, "What beautiful music-paper you use! Pray, where do you get it?" On being pressed for an opinion on a new setting of Schiller's "Lay of the Bell," he observed to the composer, "Yes, I have always thought this 'Glocke' of Schiller's one of the greatest poems ever written, and I shall continue to hold that opinion." One is reminded of Beethoven's remark to Paër on his opera "Eleonora." "What a fine libretto! I shall set it to music one of these days." It seems likely that time will confirm his estimate of Raff, concerning whom it is reported that Brahms said, on being informed that a monument was to be erected to that composer, "A monument to Raff? Dear me! Well, you had better be quick about it, lest he should be forgotten before you have got it ready."

No one sees more clearly than Brahms the harm that is done to modern composers by the fashion of commissioning works for festivals or other occasions of the kind. He has never consented to hurry his work or to force his inspiration in order to have a particular composition brought out at a particular time. For a man in his position, and in a country where the opportunities of producing new works are far more numerous than they are with us, it may be easy to make and keep a strict rule against accepting such commissions; but in England one fears that such a plan, if generally adopted by composers, would end in their sinking to the level of song-writers and purveyors of pianoforte pieces. For it is notorious that almost the only encouragement at present offered for the composition of large works of any kind comes from the committees of the autumnal festivals. That Brahms is perfectly right, however, in his disapproval of the arrangement will, I think, be felt by all earnest musicians. The caustic reply he sent to the

Leeds committee in 1887, when asked to write a work for the festival, has been printed at full length in "The History of the Leeds Festival" by Alderman Spark and Mr. Joseph Bennett, but I may be forgiven for referring to it again. He says: "Should you deem one of my old works worthy the honour of being performed on this occasion, it would be a great pleasure to me. But if this is, as it appears, not the case, how may I hope that I shall succeed this time? If, however, the charm of novelty be an absolute necessity, then pardon me if I confess that I fail properly to appreciate, or have no sympathy with, such a distinction."

If but a few of his contemporaries have excited his admiration, he yields to none in his devotion to the giants of music who have passed away. Bach is his favourite among these; and a story is told which illustrates his feeling for that master. Brahms took some friends to dine at a certain restaurant in Vienna, where the host, when asked to produce his best wine, remarked: "Here is a wine that surpasses all others as much as the music of Brahms does that of other composers." "Well, then," said Brahms, "take it away, and bring us *a bottle of Bach!*" For Haydn, too, he has a specially warm affection,

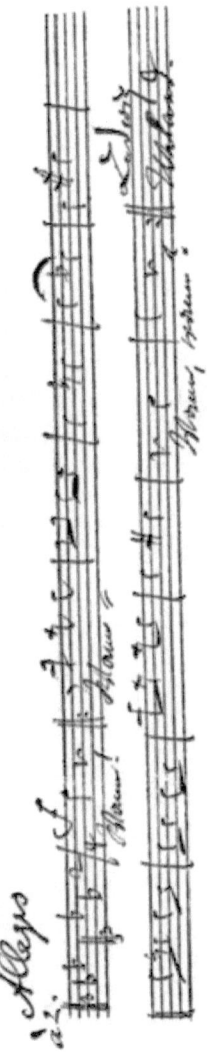

AUTOGRAPH CANON BY BRAHMS HITHERTO UNPUBLISHED

(Inserted by kind permission of the composer, and of G. Milner-Gibson-Cullum, Esq., the owner of the original.)

and a considerable part of his working hours is passed in the analysis of such models of form as this master's symphonies; his "hero-worship" of Beethoven goes so far that one of his favourite resorts is the old restaurant in the Wildmarkt where Beethoven used to dine. In his large music-library is a special "museum" devoted to autographs of the great masters, among them those of Mozart's G minor symphony, Schubert's "Wanderer," etc.

It is difficult to answer in a few words, and without help from musical illustrations, the question, What are the most striking characteristics of Brahms' music, taken as a whole? Many of its prominent peculiarities are curiously like those of Beethoven's music massive power in dealing with themes beautifully invented, or, as the phrase goes, happily "inspired;" the greatest possible degree of originality, not sought out as an end in itself, but reached as if unconsciously; and, closely connected with this last, an absolute indifference to what the pedants may think of the ultimate result, together with a certain disregard for neat and elaborate finish. One of the most personal "notes" of Brahms is his fondness for out-of-the-way rhythms, and in particular for those which are variations upon the normal triple time. The spreading of the triplet over two bars of "three-four" time, a device which occurs so strikingly in the *finale* of Schumann's piano concerto, and which is so graphically used in a passage of Brahms' "Schicksalslied," has, nowadays, very little claim to be considered as an eccentricity at all, for it is a main feature of compositions so far from recondite as the waltz in Gounod's "Faust," the once hackneyed "Il Bacio," and the refrain of "Sweethearts." But far more daring experiments have been made by Brahms, and scarcely one of his larger works does not contain instances of cross rhythms and elaborate syncopations used with consummate skill and with almost uniform success. Nowhere in the whole range of his works are they entirely absent, from the scherzo and finale of his first sonata to the "Capriccio" in D minor from op. 116, where a perfectly new cross-accent appears in the middle section. Here it is of scarcely more obvious advantage—at least if judged by the ear alone—than some of Schumann's elaborate experiments of the same kind, such as a well-known passage in the first allegro of the "Faschingsschwank aus Wien," where what appears complicated to the player or the reader of the music seems perfectly straightforward to the ear.

That his rhythms do not always spell themselves out before the hearer is, no doubt, one cause of the undeniable want of universal admiration for Brahms' work. Even among cultivated musicians there are those who still hesitate to give him the foremost place among living composers. There is nothing new or astonishing in this, for he is only undergoing what Bach Mozart, and Beethoven underwent in their own day. The non-appreciation of the greatest genius by its own contemporaries is the commonest of all incidents in the history of every art, and it has probably never happened yet that the greatest living creative artist in any department has been universally recognised by his contemporaries as even belonging to the first rank at all. Supreme achievement has always had to wait for its reward, and history shows us example after example, which should prove, to those who can argue from facts, that the universal homage and admiration of a man's contemporaries is the strongest of all arguments against his retaining the supremacy after his death. There are, of course, exceptions both ways, and it would be absurd to base a man's claim to immortality merely on the circumstance that the generation in which he lived would have none of him. But it is well to remember—in case public opinion is quoted as against the claims of a contemporary—that during the lifetime of all who are now enthroned among the immortals by common consent, the full and universal admiration which is now their right was denied them. There are undoubtedly qualities in Brahms which are likely to delay his wide appreciation by the great public even longer than usual. A close analogy might be instituted between his music and the poetry of Browning. With both of them the thought is of paramount importance, the manner of its expression a secondary thing. The idea or motive of the poem, the theme of the music, are nearly always of great and incontestable beauty; but some rhyme or turn of expression that seems clumsy to ears accustomed to the honeyed cadences of Tennyson, some harmonic or rhythmical change that strikes admirers of Mendelssohn as ungainly, comes in almost as if intent on preventing the piece from making an impression of connected beauty. There is beauty there, if we will but see it; but it is not of a kind that wins our heart at once. Nor is it easy to grasp the general drift of the poem or the musical creation at first, or, indeed, until after they have been assiduously studied. If there is no parellel among the musician's productions to the poet's virtually insoluble riddle of "Sordello," there are many compositions more or less like it, in that passages of exquisite and easily intelligible beauty are continually jostled by others of which the purpose and meaning are far from clear. To push the analogy further would be to lose sight of the thousand melodies of perfect symmetry and haunting beauty that occur in Brahms' music, and find only rare counterparts in Browning's lyrics. Of both one thing is certainly true—that the better they are known the more deeply they are loved, and the more extraordinary it seems that any person of normal intelligence and the usual educational endowment should fail to understand and admire them. Both, again, have the priceless quality that you never leave off delighting in them, when once you have learnt to love them. "How they brought the good news to Ghent" might be constantly recited at village entertainments, or Brahms' cradle-song might be as incessantly performed as Mascagni's intermezzo; one could never lose the sense of graphic power in the vigorous poem, or of perfect beauty of expression in the simple song.

It is the fashion to sneer at acquired tastes, as though these were less deeply seated than natural or congenital preferences; it will generally be found, however, that those which are formed late remain the longest and the strongest, and if we must admit that many admirers of the great German master have been only gradually awakened to the sense of the beauty of his work, there is no reason why we should suspect that their feeling for it is wanting in depth, sincerity, or permanence. Anything that is original in the highest sense, whether in itself or in its modes of expression, must be approached by all but exceptionally far-sighted persons, with a certain degree of humility. That it does not strike the ordinary amateur as beautiful at the first moment is not a sufficient reason for him to declare himself on the side of the professed opponents of the artist who has produced it. In music, a larger share of diffidence is to be desired than almost anywhere else. A picture stays on the wall, to be looked at; a poem can be read over and over till its meaning is grasped; but a musical composition passes with the moment of performance, and a man who should be able to take in all the salient points of a symphony at a first hearing and without the full score before him is scarcely to be imagined. This would hold good of a composition in a style already familiar: for instance, if Sir George Grove can unearth the "Gastein" symphony of Schubert, in the existence of which he is probably the only believer, it will be difficult enough to follow it with the ear alone, although we may have Schubert's modes of expression at our fingers' ends; how much more difficult is it, then, to expect that we can at once grasp a new work by the most original thinker among living composers, and form a trustworthy opinion upon it after a single hearing! Perhaps the most essential thing of all for a rapid realisation of Brahms' ways of working, is a keen sense of rhythm—such a sense as will allow the balance of accentuation to be (perhaps unconsciously) perceived throughout all the mutations in which the composer may indulge. In one important respect the German musician is a good deal more fortunate than the English poet: there exists no "Brahms Society," nor is there need for one, since there is, happily, no want of recognition of the composer on the part of those who make up our concert programmes. English audiences hear his most recent compositions, as a matter of course, almost as soon as they are published, and if there really exists a clique for the admiration of Brahms it is a clique that is large and rich enough to make it worth while for *entrepreneurs* of concerts to place his works in the front rank of attraction.

The word *entrepreneur* suggests the single musical form in which Brahms has not made any experiment; in every other he has given to the world compositions which will last while music lasts, but in opera he has not only done nothing, but the history of his life contains no such attempts to begin upon one as were made, for example, by Mendelssohn. So much of vigorous dramatic imagination, such buoyant humour, such romantic feeling for what is called "atmosphere," such command of "local colour," appear scattered up and down his vocal compositions, that it is difficult to believe that the stage would not appeal very strongly to him, or that he would not welcome the opportunity of dealing with a story more extensive than any of those which have suggested his more dramatic ballads. We may presume the usual difficulty of finding a good libretto to exist in his case, as it did with so many of the great composers ; but beyond this there are, or seem to be, reasons which justify the master's abstention from a form of art which presents far more temptation to a German than to an English composer, since in Germany native dramatic music is a good deal less churlishly treated by managers and audiences than is the case with us. In the present state of the stage, even in the reformed conditions begun at Bayreuth, a certain element of superficiality is hardly separable from successful operatic work; the paint and tinsel of the theatre seem to require a corresponding garishness in the music, and the highest musical creations can hardly fail to seem slightly profaned by the associations of the stage. Wagner was so many things besides a composer that he could make his own conditions and create new surroundings, and a new dramatic method in which it is difficult to see any banality whatever; but to attain the complete fulfilment of his ideal took him the whole of a fairly long life, and Brahms, we may be quite sure, would not be likely to adopt the Wagnerian methods of expressing himself in music. For one thing, form—meaning by the word constructive beauty of the highest kind—has always been dear to him, and while amplifying and modifying the moulds handed down by the classical masters he has never attempted to recast them *de novo*, as Liszt did with very imperfect success. And form, as Brahms understands it, could hardly be transferred to the theatre without results that would be unconvincing, if not actually ridiculous. Besides, the ordinary exigencies of theatrical management are so foreign to his nature that any attempt either to accommodate himself to them, or to set them at naught, is almost foredoomed to failure. Not even on his death-bed can we imagine Brahms being intimidated by a charming *prima donna*, as Goetz was, into cutting out a great concerted piece in order to leave room for a clap-trap waltz; and it is scarcely easier to conceive of a composer not accused of insusceptibility adopting the Handelian method and holding the singer out of the window until she became compliant.

The following saying of his is currently reported: "Had I already written one opera, I would assuredly have written a second; but I cannot make up my mind to write the first. I regard opera-writing (for myself) in much the same view as I do matrimony."

Whatever the future may have in store in the

way of new compositions by Brahms, we are justified by experience in expecting that they will be in no way inferior either in conception or in workmanship to those which **he** has given us already, **and in** no respect unworthy of the great position **he holds** in the estimation of the most thoughtful musicians of his own and other countries.

CATALOGUE OF PUBLISHED COMPOSITIONS BY BRAHMS.

Op.
1. Sonata, pf., in C.
2. Sonata, pf., in F sharp minor.
3. 6 Songs.
4. Scherzo, pf., in E flat minor.
5. Sonata, pf., in F minor.
6. 6 Songs.
7. 6 Songs.
8. **Trio, pf.** & strings, **in** B (afterwards issued in a revised form).
9. Variations, pf., on a theme by Schumann.
10. 4 Balladen, pf.
11. Serenade, orch., in D.
12. Ave Maria, female choir and orch.
13. Begräbnissgesang, choir and wind.

Op.
14. 8 Songs.
15. Concerto, pf. & orch., in D minor.
16. Serenade, small orch., in A.
17. 3 Songs (trios) for female choir with 2 horns and harp.
18. Sextet, **strings, in B flat.**
19. 5 Songs.
20. 3 Duets, **soprano & alto.**
21. Variations, pf., 2 sets.
22. 7 Marienlieder, choir.
23. Variations, pf., 4 hands, on a theme by Schumann.
24. Variations and fugue, pf., on a theme by Handel.
25. Quartet, pf. & strings, in G minor.
26. Quartet, pf. & strings, in A.
27. Psalm xxiii., female choir and organ.
28. 4 Duets, alto and baritone.
29. 2 Motets, 5-part choir.
30. Geistliches Lied, 4-part choir and organ.
31. **3** Vocal quartets.
32. 9 Songs.
33. **15 Romances, from Tieck's " Magelone."**
34. Quintet, pf. & strings, in F minor.
34*bis*. Sonata for 2 pfs. **arranged from** the quintet.
35. Studies, pf. (variations on a theme by Paganini).
36. Sextet, strings, in G.
37. 3 Geistliche Chöre, female choir.
38. Sonata, pf. & violoncello, in E minor.
39. Walzer, pf.
40. **Trio, pf., violin, and horn, in E flat.**
41. 5 Songs, **4-part male choir.**
42. 3 Songs, 6-part choir.

JOHANNES BRAHMS

Op.
43. 4 Songs.
44. 12 Lieder & Romanzen, female choir.
45. Ein deutsches Requiem, soli, choir, and orch.
46. 4 Songs.
47. 5 Songs.
48. 7 Songs.
49. 5 Songs.
50. Rinaldo, tenor solo, male choir, and orch.
51. 2 String quartets, in C minor and A minor.
52. Liebeslieder-Walzer, pf. (4 hands), with 4 voices *ad lib.*
53. Rhapsodie, alto solo, male choir, and orch.
54. Schicksalslied, choir and orch.
55. Triumphlied, 8-part choir and orch.
56. Variations, orch., on a theme by Haydn.
57. 8 Songs.
58. 8 Songs.
59. 8 Songs.
60. Quartet, pf. and strings, in C minor.
61. 4 Duets, soprano and alto.
62. 7 Songs for choir.
63. 9 Songs.
64. 3 Vocal quartets.
65. Neue Liebeslieder-Walzer, pf. 4-hands, with 4 voices *ad lib.*
66. 5 duets, soprano, & alto.
67. String quartet, in B flat.
68. Symphony, in C minor.
69. 9 Songs.
70. 4 Songs.
71. 5 Songs.

Op.
- 72. 5 Songs.
- 73. Symphony, in D.
- 74. 2 Motets, choir.
- 75. 4 Vocal duets.
- 76. 8 Clavierstücke (Capricci & Intermezzi).
- 77. Concerto, vln. and orch., in D.
- 78. Sonata, pf. & vln., in G.
- 79. 2 Rhapsodies, pf.
- 80. Akademische Festouvertüre.
- 81. Tragische Ouvertüre.
- 82. Nänie (Schiller), choir and orch.
- 83. Concerto, pf. and orch., in B flat.
- 84. 5 Songs (for one or two voices).
- 85. 6 Songs.
- 86. 6 Songs.
- 87. Trio, pf. & strings, in C.
- 88. String quintet, in F.
- 89. Gesang der Parzen, 6-part choir and orch.
- 90. Symphony in E.
- 91. 2 Songs, alto with viola obbligato.
- 92. 4 Vocal Quartets.
- 93A. 6 Songs for choir.
- 93B. Tafellied, 6.pt. choir.
- 94. 5 Songs.
- 95. 7 Songs.
- 96. 4 Songs.
- 97. 6 Songs.
- 98. Symphony in E minor.
- 99. Sonata, pf. & violoncello, in F.
- 100. Sonata, pf. & vln., in A.
- 101. Trio, pf. & strings, in C minor.

JOHANNES BRAHMS

Op.
102. Concerto, vln. & vcello. with orch., in C.
103. Zigeunerlieder, 7 vocal quartets.
104. 5 Songs, choir.
105. 5 Songs.
106. 5 Songs.
107. 5 Songs.
108. Sonata, pf. & vln., in D minor.
109. Fest- & Gedenksprüche, 3 motets, 8-part choir.
110. 3 Motets, choir.
111. String quintet, in G.
112. 6 Vocal quartets.
113. Canons, female choir.
114. Trio, pf., clar. & vcello., in A minor.
115. Quintet, clar. & strings, in B minor.
116. 8 Fantasien (Capricci & Intermezzi), pf.
117. 3 Intermezzi, pf.
118. 6 Clavierstücke, pf.
119. 4 Clavierstücke, pf.

Works without opus-numbers:—
Abendregen. (Blätter für Hausmusik.)
Chorale Prelude for organ, on "O Traurigkeit, o Herzeleid."
Deutsche Volkslieder. 14 Songs.
Fugue, organ, in A flat minor.
Gavotte, by Gluck, arranged for pf.
Song; Mondnacht.
5 Studies, pf.
Ungarische Tänze, pf. 4 hands, 4 books.
51 Uebungen, pf.

MAX BRUCH

It is not easy to estimate the exact distance which separates him whom the wisest critics call the greatest of living German composers from the master whom most of these would agree in placing nearest to him in order of artistic merit; nor is it likely that if the relative greatness of the two could be assessed, all or even the majority of those whose opinion is best worth having would measure it in the same way. They would, I think, agree in one thing: that a very great interval should be placed between MAX BRUCH and the rest of his German contemporaries. For my own part I should not hesitate to place Bruch midway between Brahms and the other composers of their country, and to make both intervals wide. It is especially difficult for English people to realise what a power Bruch's music is in Germany, and how popular, in the best sense, it is, since the composer spent some time in England and was received with a coolness which we most rarely exhibit to musicians of other nations. Very little of his music has entered into what may be called the permanent repertory of English concerts, and the works that have attained to the dignity of standard compositions with us do not belong to the class in which Bruch's widest fame has been won. That neither the composer nor his work has found real acceptance in the English musical world must be admitted by all who are acquainted with his compositions as a whole. It is certainly not the fault of the compositions, since these, or the best of them at all events, are distinguished by great and easily intelligible beauty, and by the rare quality of distinction.

In dubbing him "echt niederrheinisch," a German wit went no further than the truth. Both the music and the man belong to the Lower Rhine country by every circumstance of origin and congenital disposition. The broadly flowing melodies of his invention suggest the course of such a river as that of his native country, and the absence of any very great heights in his music might be held to support the analogy. Born at Cologne, January 6,

1838, he is the grandson of a once-famous clergyman of the Evangelical Church at Cologne, Dr. Christian Bruch; his father held a high official position in the same town, and his mother had sung with success, under her maiden name of Almenräder, at many of the Lower Rhine festivals. She was her son's first music teacher, and taught him to such excellent purpose that by the time he was fourteen a symphony of his was considered worthy of being performed by the Cologne Philharmonic Society. This symphony was only one of some seventy compositions in all branches of music produced by the young composer since his first attempts at the age of nine. In the year made memorable to him by the performance of his symphony, he won the exhibition (Stipendium), worth 400 gulden annually for four years, of the "Mozart Stiftung" at Frankfort, one of the judges being Spohr. The award led to his being placed under the tuition of Ferdinand Hiller, with whom he remained until 1861, with the single exception of a short visit to Leipzig in 1858, where he came in contact with Moscheles, Hauptmann, David, and others. He made a longer tour after the death of his father in 1861, and ultimately settled down at

Mannheim, where he lived from 1862 to 1864. Both the journeys mentioned were undertaken (the second partly for the sake of health, for signs of overwork were showing themselves) at the suggestion of Hiller, whose almost parental care was richly rewarded by his pupil's success both as a composer and a conductor. In the latter capacity he appeared fairly regularly at many of the Rhineland centres of music.

It is not many composers whose first numbered or acknowledged work is in operatic form, or who first have attracted public attention by a dramatic work. It is possibly due to the enormous number of Bruch's early attempts in different forms that he acquired the ease and assured command of structure which are the most remarkable features of his op. 1, an opera in one act, "Scherz, List und Rache," written to the libretto which Goethe intended, it is said, for Ditters von Dittersdorf. The opera by which his name first became known resembled this in one particular, that its "book" was at first intended for another composer. Mendelssohn's difficulties in procuring an operatic libretto are familiar to all who know his life, and when at last he got from Geibel a poem in three acts on the Lorelei legend, he did not live to finish more than a very few numbers. This book the poet steadily refused to give to any other composer; but, notwithstanding this, Bruch, who read it when it was first published separately in 1861, had the resolution to undertake its composition; and one of the main objects of his journey in that year was to break down, if he might, the restrictions of Geibel, who was then living at Munich. He attained his object, and the opera, carefully prepared by Vincenz Lachner, the conductor of the opera at Mannheim, was produced there on June 14, 1863. The success it achieved was not confirmed when it was given on some of the other principal stages of Germany, and, only three years after its first appearance, its performance at Mainz was noticed in one of the papers under the heading "Accidents." In later years the composer entirely re-cast his work, and Oscar Walther, of the Leipzig opera-house, made a new arrangement of the libretto, compressing its four acts into three, and making other important changes. As an instance of how thorough were the alterations made, it may be mentioned that the passage which is well-known as the finale of Mendelssohn's fragment appears, according to the first version of Bruch's opera, in the second act, while in the newer version it is delayed until the last act. In its new guise the work was brought out at Leipzig in 1887, and made a *succès d'estime;* even in its altered form the story was too weak and invertebrate an affair to make a lasting success likely; it is not often that amended versions of serious operas excite much enthusiasm, and this was no exception to the rule. There is a danger in choosing for stage-presentment a story that is too familiar, and, seeing that the legend of this opera has been used *usque ad nauseam* in every sort of art, both in Germany and elsewhere, there was the less chance of its proving really successful, unless a far more dramatic libretto had been provided for it than the poem which Geibel put together. The music contains many beautiful numbers, notably the large *ensembles,* the fine chorus which begins the second act, formerly the third, and the picturesque chorus of Rhine spirits with the dramatic soprano solo, which formerly was the whole second act, and now appears as the finale of the opera. One obvious difficulty to the composer was the result of taking a libretto which a predecessor had begun to set—namely, that of avoiding resemblances which in this case would have been particularly easy to identify, since Mendelssohn's fragment is sufficiently well known. It is to Bruch's credit that he did avoid such resemblances completely. He must have had intuition enough to perceive, in spite of the temporary success of his opera, that the stage was not the best sphere for his talent, for he made no further essay in dramatic composition for some time to come, until he had, indeed, "found his feet" in a form of music which he had already cultivated with success. While the fifteen numbered compositions preceding the "Loreley" in his list contain pianoforte duet and solos, a trio, and two string quartets, beside vocal works for solo or chorus, the group of works which separate his opera from his next composition of great importance are exclusively vocal. He attained, whether by this or other means, to the complete ease in writing for the voice which characterises much of his best work. He seems to have contemplated some large "Christmas oratorio" or the like, for his ops. 20 and 21 deal respectively with the Flight into Egypt and the Visit of the three Kings. This last is immediately succeeded by his op. 23, the famous "Frithjof Scenen," for male chorus, soli, and orchestra: for, by an oversight, the number 22 was left out, and has never been filled up. The words—by Esaias Tegner, the well-known Swedish poet—exactly suit Bruch's free, open-air manner, and it was little wonderful that the scenes attained a real and lasting success immediately upon their first appearance under the composer's direction at Aix-la-Chapelle. The recognition the work at once obtained may be best illustrated, not by quoting a list of the German performances given within the first few years after its production, but by mentioning the fact that it reached Paris in the following year, and was no less successful there than it had been in its native land. The composer, who conducted it, made friends with Rossini and Berlioz, both of whom were among the warm admirers of his composition, a circumstance which points at once to the obvious character of its melody, and to the originality of its conception. Already, at the age of twenty-six, Bruch had acquired an extraordinary power and facility in the manipulation of large vocal masses; his choral writing, while entirely free from pedantry or stiffness of any kind, was even now the work of a completely accomplished musician, solid and earnest as well as spontaneous, tuneful and effective. Although he has since written worthy companion pieces to the "Frithjof Scenen" he has not yet produced one that throws this early work into the shade, nor is he likely to do so. The six scenes chosen from the "Frithjof saga" of Tegner are treated with a genuine dramatic feeling which is scarcely ever revealed in the "Loreley;" the masterly treatment of the third of these, in which Frithjof avenges the loss of Ingeborg, is most remarkable; the fourth, "Frithjof's Farewell," is admirably laid out for effect, and the pathetic processional music of the unwilling bride, and her "lament" in the fifth scene, are exceedingly expressive. The last was at one time familiar in English concert-rooms, but the work as a whole, though given with success at a Crystal Palace concert, June 8, 1878, has fallen into quite undeserved neglect. Two other choral works, opp. 24 and 25, and a third, "Frithjof auf seines Vaters Grabhügel," a concert scena for baritone, female choir, and orchestra, which is no doubt to be regarded as a kind of appendix to the scenes, were the next compositions in order of publication; but meanwhile changes had taken place in Bruch's outward circumstances. In the autumn of 1865 he went to Coblenz as conductor of the concert-institution there, and, after a year and a half of work in this capacity, he was appointed court-capellmeister to the Prince of Schwarzburg-Sondershausen. Just as Brahms' tenure of a similar post at the Court of Lippe-Detmold gave him experience in choral-writing, so these appointments brought Bruch into relations of a closer kind than he would otherwise have enjoyed with an admirable orchestra, the outcome of which intimacy may be seen in the first violin concerto in G minor and the two symphonies in E flat and F minor respectively. The choral works mentioned above were also written at Sondershausen. The first, " Schön Ellen " (first performed at Leipzig in 1869), is set to a poem by Geibel, who transferred to the more romantic surroundings of the Scotland of romance the apocryphal episode of the siege of Lucknow, according to which a girl brought hope to the exhausted defenders of the city by declaring that she heard the pipes playing "The Campbells are coming." This tune has no very romantic associations for English hearers, and it is no wonder that no performance has yet been given here of a work which makes so large a use of a melody not among the best of Scottish tunes. For other audiences it is, no doubt, impressive enough, and its distinctly happy employment of local colour, apart from the tune referred to, is extremely good. Considering that the composer had devoted some time while at Mannheim to the study of national music of all sorts, and having regard to the fact that he arranged a set of twelve Scottish songs that were practically unknown and very beautiful, it is only natural that he should have been attracted to this poem by the man whose "Loreley" he had set but a few years ago. A very beautiful number is the solo, "Fahrt wohl denn, Weib und Kind daheim," for baritone, which, with the soprano, is the only single voice employed. The chorus is "mixed" in this work, the male choir alone being employed in the other cantata, "Salamis," a fine and energetic song of victory, belonging to a class of subjects especially dear to the composer, who, like the young man in Mr. Kipling's "Finest Story in the World," is never so much in his element as in Greek or Scandinavian stories of heroism and adventure, more especially by sea.

The violin concerto already mentioned, in G minor, op. 26, though written at Coblenz, was not published until after these two cantatas had appeared. It is dedicated to Joachim, and bears upon it the impress of his character and genius in every movement. Grave and earnest from beginning to end, yet rising into passionate outbursts of almost tragic intensity, this work acquired at once a place of its own among violin concertos. Its melodies have a character deeper, nobler, and more genuinely expressive than any former work of its composer's, and its solo part is written with consummate knowledge of violin effect. If it hardly deserves to be reckoned, as some critics have done, among the three greatest concertos for the instrument, beside those of Beethoven and Mendelssohn, it comes, at all events, as one of the first five—that is to say, it is only equalled by two more works of the kind—the concerto of Brahms, and the exquisite "Hungarian" concerto of Joachim. The first two movements are so rich in lovely thoughts charmingly expressed, that the finale makes, perhaps, less effect than it otherwise would; and it seems, indeed, as if in the romance the composer's vein of inspiration was for the time exhausted. For none of the large group of works, numbered 28 to 40, come up to the standard of his best compositions, although they include church-music—a motet, "Rorate Cœli," and portions of a mass—the two symphonies already mentioned, and several more short choral pieces, among them a beautiful setting of Schiller's "Dithyrambe." "Das Lied vom Deutschen Kaiser" was his tribute to the Imperial triumph after the Franco-German war, and it was shortly afterwards followed by a four-act opera, "Hermione," based on "The Winter's Tale," by a librettist named Hoppfer. This was produced in Berlin in 1872, but, from much the same cause as the former theatrical failure, met with no very remarkable degree of success. It contains some well-written instrumental numbers, which might be very effective if arranged as a suite for orchestra.

In the previous year Bruch had given up his Court appointment in order to devote himself more exclusively to composition, and the work that succeeds the opera in the catalogue is that by which Bruch's name is, perhaps, best known all the world over. Again he reached his highest point in setting to music isolated scenes from a story that appealed strongly to his imagination, and there can be no doubt that the "Odyssey" lends itself particularly well to this sort of treatment, since its episodes are fairly short and not too closely connected with each other. A close study of this masterpiece of Bruch's genius will shed some light on his failure as an operatic composer. Separate as the ten scenes are from each other, several of them, indeed the greater part, consist of various musical "movements," and in the transitions from one such movement to another we cannot but feel that the composer is a little constrained and, as it were, uncomfortable until he lands us in the new section. If this is the case in a work without action, how much more is it noticeable in a composition intended for the stage, where it is indispensable that the various solos and ensemble pieces should be divided, either by spoken dialogue such as has now gone out of fashion except in the lighter forms of opera, or by music more or less partaking of the character of recitative! For the "endless melody" of Wagner would hardly be adopted by a writer so little in sympathy with the modern tendencies of music as Bruch has proved himself. The Odysseus" contains numbers of such transitional passages, although they are reduced in extent as much as possible, a proceeding which makes the sections divided by them approach each other far too closely for good effect.

There are not many librettos, sacred or secular, better suited to the requirements of the composer

MAX BRUCH

for whom they are intended than this series of scenes arranged from the "Odyssey" by Herr P. W. Graff. Each is thoroughly representative and picturesque; all are in good contrast with each other, and none of the most prominent features of the story are either omitted or dwelt upon at too great length. The first, "Ulysses in the Island of Calypso," contains some charming three-part choruses for female voices, and, after a short scene between Ulysses and Hermes, who announces to him Zeus' permission that he shall return home safely, a phrase, most happily "invented," is heard, which afterwards recurs as a musical equivalent of the prosperous voyage, and the scene closes very effectively with a baritone solo. The visit to the infernal regions occupies the next division of the work; no musical picture of the darker aspects of the classical Hades is attempted, and the various episodes of Teiresias, the mother of Ulysses, and the like, are treated with a grace that a more politic composer would hardly have cared to impart to them, even if he could, for fear of discounting the effect of what was to follow. The composer justifies himself in the next number, for it loses but very little of its effect from its position, since its melodious beauty is far in excess of anything we have yet heard. The richly harmonised song of the sailors as they prepare to resist the sirens' sweet sounds, throw these into stronger relief when they are heard, and the scene is throughout of magical beauty. That it would have been more effective still if we had been allowed to taste some of the horror which should at least appear in the previous scene, can hardly be denied. In the fourth scene we have a vigorous description of a storm, culminating in a beautiful chorus of sea-nymphs with Leucothea at their head, a number which suitably ends the first part of this "secular oratorio," as it is called. The second "act" begins with an expressive solo for Penelope (mezzo-soprano), which comes as a pleasant relief after the ensembles of the former scenes, although in itself it is not one of the most remarkable parts of the work. The pretty chorus, with solos, which follows it gives a most charming picture of Nausicaa with her maidens, and their reception of Ulysses, and the scene is an appropriate introduction to the magnificent scene of the Banquet with the Phæacians, which is rightly regarded as the climax of the work. Starting with a broadly treated song of welcome, which no one but a scientific musician would suspect of being in *fugato* form, so freely does the theme seem to be handled, the festal feeling of the scene is splendidly maintained, and the fine passage of eight-part harmony in which the Rhapsodes are called upon to sing the tale of Troy leads most brilliantly into their unisonous song, a vigorous measure in triple time. We have hardly time to take breath after this before we are plunged into another massive ensemble number, led off by Ulysses, whose tears at hearing of the deeds in which he has taken part lead to his identification. He sings of the joys of home, and the rest of the company "join in"; exquisite as the musical setting of the passage undoubtedly is, it would have been wiser to dwell on the episode of the identification—a not unimportant one, surely—a little longer, if only to allow the hearers to prepare for the suave strains in which the domestic blisses are so melodiously sung. It is thankless work, however, cavilling at what, after all, is a scene of very great beauty and power, which very few musicians of any nation could improve or rival. And the actual setting of the words in which Ulysses makes himself known, "Ich bin's, bin Odysseus selbst," is perfect in its simplicity and directness. Yet another section of massive design and beautiful workmanship, describing the resumption of the voyage, has to come, before the scene is ended. The very beautiful song of Penelope weaving her endless web, with its refrain "O kehre, Odysseus," is among the most expressive and perfectly formed of its author's creations; no wonder that it has become a standard song among German contraltos, for its poetical motive loses nothing by its performance apart from the rest, while in its place it is a little apt to escape attention, and to serve merely as a sort of *entr'acte* between two more salient sections. The final divisions, occupied with the return of Ulysses and the feast at Ithaca, rely for their effect more on the elaborate chorus of rejoicing, "Lasst Opfer flammen," than on anything else; the themes of the short duet which precedes it have appeared in important positions in the overture, and the climax of the scene with the Phæacians is resumed for the close of the whole. The repetition of this by another set of characters—for Ulysses alone is supposed to take part in both—may take away a little of what verisimilitude the scenes might have; but it is a very difficult thing to say how far such things are admissible in cantatas, though, of course, it is easy enough to see that anything of the kind would be wholly out of place on the stage. On its production at Bremen in 1873 this beautiful work was received with much enthusiasm, for it is of a kind that makes its effect immediately, though that effect is by no means transient or superficial. The success achieved by it wherever it has been given has been very remarkable, considering how completely free it is from the *ad captandum* element.

As Bruch's first violin concerto was published almost immediately after a group of his most successful choral works, so again it happened, whether by accident or design, that the beautiful work just noticed was directly followed by another violin composition for which violinists are apt to claim an equally high place with the concerto. In its necessarily smaller scale, the "Romance," op. 42, for violin and orchestra, is in no way inferior to the former work; the same perfect realisation of the best characteristics of violin music, the same broadly melodious themes treated with the same elegance and real mastery, appear in the later as in the earlier creation, and the two stand together among the highest achievements of the composer's genius. The romance was written for the late Robert Heckmann, the founder and leader of the famous string quartet called after him, but in style and character there is nothing to distinguish it from the concerto; no such difference as appears, for example, between the first and second concertos, the latter of which reflects the individuality of Sarasate (for whom it was written) as closely as the former does that of Joachim. This is far more of a bravura piece, more sentimental, more obviously written with a view to effect, than its predecessor, and in spite of its many beauties must be considered as in every way on a lower level than the other. It was written at the time when Bruch had taken up his residence at Bonn in order to enjoy complete leisure for composition It may be that the coquettish quality which we call inspiration may have declined to favour the composer's suit just because he had so carefully laid out his life in order to court it. The so-called "oratorio" of "Arminius" dates from the same time. Dedicated to Mr. Henschel, it contains a very fine baritone part; the six-part choruses, "Ich habe sie geseh'n;" and that which accompanies the death of Siegmund, are impressive and excellently worked, and the whole is concise and certainly effective in many

FACSIMILE OF AUTOGRAPH SCORE BY MAX BRUCH

ways. The reason for employing the female choir as well as the male in the numbers supposed to be sung by Roman soldiers is not very evident, and of course the practice does not add to the realism of these sections.

Far better than this is the setting of Schiller's "Lied von der Glocke,"* a work which also dates from the Bonn period, but is certainly one of his best as well as most popular productions. It is not an easy thing, in spite of the many obvious suggestions which the poem offers to musicians, to give it the necessary variety, or to apportion it successfully between solo voices and choir; this difficulty has been overcome by Bruch with remarkable success, and the work cannot certainly be reproached with any lack of effect. The introductory chorus, "Vivos voco," the first baritone solo with its broadly flowing phrases; the pretty chorus, "Denn mit der Freude Feierklänge," with its fine organ prelude; the charming love-passages, "O zarte Sehnsucht," and the stirring fine chorus which leads so charmingly to the tranquil ensemble "Ein süsser Trost," give to the first part an interest and attraction

* It may, perhaps, be worth mentioning that it was not Bruch's setting of this poem that called forth the caustic sneer from Brahms, quoted on p. 78.

above the second, though the chorus, "Heil'ge Ordnung," and the finale, are admirably worked numbers. Here, again, the composer is at his best when singing the joys of domestic life, and each subject, of the first part at least, suits him excellently.

The first of Bruch's visits to England took place in the autumn of 1877; the immediate object of his journey was to conduct the new violin concerto for Señor Sarasate, for whom it was specially intended. On October 13 of that year he conducted it, and the prelude to his "Loreley," at the Crystal Palace, where both were received with much favour. Ten days later he conducted the "Odysseus" at Liverpool; the work was first given in England at Manchester, March 13, 1875, with Mary Davies, Redeker, and Henschel in the principal parts. In the spring of 1878 he paid us another visit, conducting his "Frithjof" at the Crystal Palace on June 8. The performance of "Odysseus" at Liverpool belongs to this year, a somewhat momentous performance for the composer, since to its success he owed the invitation to a permanent post in that town two years later. Meanwhile his period of leisure from all but composition had come to an end, for in

1878 he succeeded Stockhausen as director of the "Gesangverein" founded by Julius Stern in Berlin. While in England he was invited to contribute a work to the Birmingham Festival of 1879; he at first intended to write a new choral cantata on the subject of "The Lady of the Lake," but whether from pressure of other work, or from any other reason, he failed to do this, and the directors of the Festival had to content themselves with giving the first English performance of "The Lay of the Bell," instead of a brand-new composition. The work succeeded with the audience, though some of the more severe critics reproached it on account of the want of interest in the narrative portions, and with want of inspiration. The composer's fame had now become sufficiently established in England to make it seem not such a very unwise thing to offer him the post of conductor of the Liverpool Philharmonic Society, on the retirement of Sir Julius Benedict, who after a fashion that is not yet quite exploded, managed to combine his Lancashire duties with the more agreeable occupations of his London life. Those who had the interests of music most at heart among the Liverpool amateurs felt that an opportunity had come for the engagement of a first-rate foreign conductor whose name was becoming well known in English musical circles, and they very properly made residence in Liverpool a condition of the appointment. Bruch had made a great impression by his conducting and by the direction of the choir on the occasions when "Odysseus" and "The Lay of the Bell" had been given by the Society. Not only were the committee, or at all events many of the most influential members, convinced of his ability, but the choristers approved of him, and those who know the constitution of our English music-meetings are aware how much that meant. In spite of his popularity with those who had most right to an opinion, there was a party, not merely in Liverpool but in the musical world of London, who opposed themselves to the appointment by every means in their power, on the plea of "Englishmen for English Music," a cry that might be reasonable enough did it not proceed as a general rule from those who are most tolerant of foreign incapables, and busiest in ignoring such English talent as may declare itself, whether in composition or in any other branch of artistic activity. It has often been pointed out how very little we should know of the most advanced and original of the compositions of the younger English school, as well as of the treasures of the glorious English schools of the past, if the work of foreigners in bringing them forward could be entirely taken away. Things are better now, it is true, and there are many Englishmen who have a right to be considered as protectors of native art; but in the seventies it was not so, and, besides this, it would have been difficult to find an Englishman really fitted for such an appointment as was offered to Bruch, at least among those musicians who were not already fully occupied in other ways. The cry was all the more absurd, too, since Bruch's predecessor was also a German by birth. Bruch was of a far less sensitive fibre than the somewhat apocryphal Keats whom the "Scotch reviewer" snuffed out, and he was not the man to abandon the good work that he found waiting for him to do because the musical critics set themselves against him: this was not why he resigned the appointment, after holding it for two years and a half. By the kindness of Mr. H. E. Rensburg, of Liverpool, I am able to give the main reasons for his departure from England in the spring of 1883. The members of the choir of the Society had even more than the usual amount of voice in its arrangements, since they were in some sort its founders, and as such were largely represented on its committee; Bruch's attitude to them was at the root of the strained relations which soon began to appear, as it had been one of the chief causes of his appointment. Perhaps if he had adhered to the old arrangement by which a choirmaster was responsible for the ordinary work of rehearsals, things might have gone more smoothly, though the performances might have suffered; this arrangement, though doubtless very convenient to Benedict, did not at all suit the thoroughgoing nature of his successor, and he very soon abolished the choirmaster, conducting the practices in person with the aid of an accompanist. For a time all went well, and it has never been contested that the standard of performance given under the new management was very much higher than it had been; the unity of control yielded good results immediately, and the welcome given by the public of Liverpool was a most hearty and hospitable one. No doubt Bruch's popularity with his choir would have lasted longer than it did if he had been able to speak English fluently; the best conductor is not always the most popular, however, and it is not to be expected that members of the class from which choral societies are usually recruited should give their due value to the details of artistic excellence, or weigh them against any little jars such as must always arise between a conductor and his choir, unless indeed he is exceptionally diplomatic or exceptionally easygoing. Bruch happens to be neither the one nor the other, but to possess most keen artistic feelings and intolerance of anything short of perfection in performance. While his imperfect English made his dealings with the choir more difficult than they otherwise might have been, it had another effect—that of withdrawing him from what there was of cultivated society outside the necessarily limited circle of German residents; and this was naturally a serious loss to a man who had enjoyed to the full his intercourse with the intellectual aristocracy of his own country.

If the best fruits of his residence in England are to be sought in the improved standard of performances in the Liverpool Society, and if no very great composition of his dates from the time when he was living among us, the episode had one important result for him, since it was at Liverpool that he married Fräulein Clara Tuczek; and to lovers of English music it is not uninteresting to know that, while at Liverpool, Bruch gave lessons in orchestration to the late Arthur Goring Thomas. The group of works written at Liverpool includes a set of three Hebrew melodies for choir and orchestra, several times brought forward at the concerts of the society; the "Scottish Fantasia" for violin and orchestra, a work which illustrates very happily the composer's singular affinity with a certain class of national music, but one which at its first production did not attain the success it has since made; a quintet for piano and strings, which does not appear in the numbered list of his works; and the famous violoncello piece "Kol Nidrei," founded on a subject of Hebrew origin, still in use in the synagogue ritual. Would it be unreasonable to see in the inexpressibly sad strains of this beautiful little work a reflection of the state of the writer's feelings at the time, conscious, at all events, of partial failure, and of want of appreciation, with possibly some trace of home-sickness? It was "a far cry" from the Rhine to the Mersey, from the storied river beside which he had lived practically all his life, to the commercial surroundings which were only too faithfully reflected in the minds of many with whom he was brought in contact: is it any wonder that he longed to get away, or that he ultimately gave up the post?

Besides the conductorship of this society, Bruch held that of another choral body, formed by the amalgamation of two choirs of long standing. This has now practically superseded the former Liverpool Philharmonic chorus. A performance of "Odysseus," given in March 1883 by the Bach Choir, was conducted by the composer, who during his residence in Liverpool received many offers from various parts of the world. That he refused them shows that his life at Liverpool was not throughout an irksome one. An offer of a conductorship at New York, though it was not accepted, may have led to the tour in the United States which he undertook in April and May 1883. In the summer of that year he was back in Germany, and in September he became conductor of the orchestral society at Breslau.

Since his return to his own country he has given to the world several compositions that are worthy of his genius in its highest development. The most prominent of these is, undoubtedly, the "Achilleus," which was evidently intended to be a companion work to the "Odysseus," and which fulfils that intention in the best possible way. In structure it is even better than the earlier work; the recitative-like passages which separate the sections are a good deal stronger and more spontaneous than those of "Odysseus," and add greatly to the general effect; the scenes themselves are treated with the same picturesque feeling, the same breadth of melody, and the same free swing that appear in the other. Yet it would be perhaps too much to say that it is in all respects its equal; the earlier production surpasses the later in the originality of its ideas and in freshness of treatment. The libretto, arranged from the "Iliad" by Herr H. Bulthaupt, consists of three parts or acts, in which are successively described the discussions in the Greek camp as to the continuation or abandonment of the siege, the parting of Hector and Andromache, the fight between Achilles and Hector, the triumph of the former suggesting a brilliant song of victory for the end of the second part; the third opens with the funeral games in honour of the dead Patroclus, a most interesting and effective group of numbers, containing three elaborate quasi-ballet movements; the lamentation of the widowed Andromache, in some ways forming a counterpart to the songs of Penelope in the earlier work, and a scene in which Priam begs for the restoration of his son's body, lead to an epilogue in which the chorus alludes more or less directly to the death of Achilles himself. The most striking numbers, beside the pantomime music already mentioned, which, by the way, was given under the composer's direction at one of the Philharmonic Concerts of last season, and with great success, are the prologue for six-part choir, the five sections in which Achilles is consoled by his mother, Thetis, after the death of Patroclus—scenes in which the most attractive side of the composer's power is displayed—an elaborate "Morgengesang" for quartet and chorus, the number in which the fight is described, and in which the utterances of the Greeks and Trojans as they watch the issue are admirably combined and contrasted, and the beautiful funeral chorus "Durch die ambrosische Nacht." The solos of Achilles and, in fact, all the solo parts, are interesting and expressive, well designed and carried out, and it is rather surprising that no choral society in England has yet had the courage to take up the work and introduce it to the public of London or the provinces. The success of the new "oratorio," when produced at Bonn in 1885 was not less than that of its predecessor; a third symphony in E (op. 51) was possibly occasioned by the Breslau appointment, which was given up in 1889. In that year he went to live in Berlin, and in the same year a new cantata appeared which it is difficult not to connect with the Birmingham suggestion of ten years before. For " Das Feuerkreuz," the book of which was prepared by Herr Bulthaupt, is founded on a short episode from the third canto of " The Lady of the Lake," and though the sorrows of Norman and "Tombea's Mary" are not expanded by Scott, the first and most suggestive scene of the cantata is due to him, that, namely, in which the marriage is interrupted by the advent of the fiery cross which the bridegroom must carry on to the next bearer. The musical setting of the piece is scarcely in Bruch's best manner, though he has not hesitated to employ such modern additions to the recognised orchestra as a bell and an organ in the church scene. The number most worthy of him is the "Kriegsge-sang," in which a march-motive is finely worked.

Among the latest of Bruch's works are a third violin concerto of great merit and brilliancy, showing a great improvement on the second, though scarcely reaching as high a point as the first; a very expressive *Adagio appassionato* for violin and orchestra, two pieces for violoncello and orchestra, some short choral pieces, among which the deeply felt "Gruss an die heilige Nacht" (with an alto solo) is the most important, an effective set of "Swedish Dances" for violin and piano, a "Scottish Fantasia" for violin, harp, and orchestra, "In Memoriam," an adagio for violin and orchestra, and a mass, some portions of which were recently performed at Barmen with great success. When we think how much of beauty and real value is comprised in what seems so short a list of works we shall realise one of the composer's best qualities, his rare amount of self-criticism, leading him to the determination to give the world nothing but what he considers his best. He is one of those who uphold most worthily the dignity of the art, and if he has not attained to the position of one whose every publication is received by musicians with the reverence due to a new revelation, he has won the hearts of many thousands of hearers by his beautiful creations in certain branches of music—viz., choral works of large design with orchestral accompaniment, and works for violin or violoncello. It is curious to see how very little lasting effect has been made by the many works in forms other than the two here referred to, while so many compositions in these two classes have won almost universal admiration. His melodies, with their broad design, seldom suit the solo voice as they do the choral; a special quality in his work is his original and individual way of disposing his harmonies, and this is exhibited far more strikingly in choral works than in any others; and his writing for orchestra alone is less spontaneous than when the instruments are used in accompanying. For this cause, partly, his symphonies do not belong to the small number of those by living composers that are likely to endure; the very extent and pronounced character of his themes—in fact just the quality that makes them so suitable for choir or solo stringed instruments—does not make them any the more pliable for those thematic developments which are, or should be, the crowning feature in symphonic work. While, too, the composer has all the resources of the orchestra at his fingers' ends, he is not of those whose treatment of the orchestra is delightful independently of the material dealt with. The matter of his utterance is always of more importance than the manner, and it is difficult to find fault with him on this account.

MAX BRUCH

That the best of his works, including among these not merely the few compositions that have become almost hackneyed, but the large number that deserve to be as well known, should not be more often heard in England or more widely appreciated by English people is one of the anomalies of our musical state at the present moment. "Kol Nidrei" is often heard at chamber concerts, and three, or at most four, of the works for violin hold a permanent place in the repertory of players, but beyond this we are allowed to hear very little of a master who certainly has deserved better things at our hands.

As a matter of course honours of all kinds have been showered upon Bruch. Numerous Prussian and Bavarian orders have been conferred upon him; he has been since 1888 a member of the Berlin Academy of Arts, and has had the title of "Professor" since 1890. In June of last year he received the honorary degree of Mus. D. from the University of Cambridge, representing Germany on that occasion, as Saint-Saëns, Boïto, and Tschaïkowsky represented France, Italy, and Russia. He conducted the banquet scene from "Odysseus" at the concert in the Guildhall, and three days later appeared at the Philharmonic concert of June 15 as before mentioned.

If a somewhat blunt manner and an amount of self-centredness that is not common even amongst musicians prevent his making friends very quickly, or being what is called popular in general society, those who know him best know how whole-hearted is his devotion to his art, how pure are his aims, and how honest and upright he is in every artistic matter, as well as in those which concern everyday life.

CATALOGUE OF PUBLISHED COMPOSITIONS BY MAX BRUCH.

Op.
1. "Scherz, List, und Rache," comic opera in one act.
2. Capriccio, pf., 4 hands.
3. "Jubilate, Amen," for soprano, choir, & orch.
4. 3 Duets, soprano and alto.
5. Trio, pf. & strings, in C minor.
6. 7 Songs, 2 and 3 part choir.
7. 6 Songs.
8. "Die Birken und die Erlen," soprano, choir, and orch.

MAX BRUCH

Op.
- 9. String quartet, in C minor.
- 10. String quartet, in E.
- 11. Fantaisie for 2 pfs.
- 12. 6 small pf. pieces.
- 13. Hymn for soprano.
- 14. 2 Pf. pieces.
- 15. 4 Songs.
- 16. " Die Loreley," grand opera in 3 acts.
- 17. 10 Songs.
- 18. 4 Songs, baritone.
- 19. 2 Sets of male-voice choruses.
- 20. " Die Flucht der heiligen Familie," choir & orch.
- 21. " Gesang der heiligen drei Könige," 3 male voices & orch.
- 22. (not written).
- 23. "Frithjof-Scenen," soli, male choir, & orch.
- 24. " Schön Ellen," soprano & baritone solos, choir, & orch.
- 25. " Salamis," male choir and orch.
- 26 Concerto, vln. & orch., in G minor.
- 27. " Frithjof auf seines Vaters Grabhügel," baritone solo, female choir, and orch.
- 28. Symphony in E flat.
- 29. " Rorate Cœli," choir, orch., & organ.
- 30. " Die Priesterin der Isis in Rom," alto & orch.
- 31. " Flucht nach Aegypten," and " Morgenstunde," soprano, female choir & orch.
- 32. " Normannenzug," baritone solo, male choir, and orch.
- 33. 4 Songs.
- 34. " Römische Leichenfeier," choir & orch.

Op.
35. Kyrie, Sanctus, and Agnus Dei, 2 soprano solos, double choir, orch., and organ.
36. Symphony in F minor.
37. "Das Lied vom Deutschen Kaiser."
38. 5 Songs for choir, *a capella*.
39. "Dithyrambe," tenor solo, 6-part choir, & orch.
40. "Hermione," grand opera in 4 acts.
41. "Odysseus," soli, choir, & orch.
42. Romance, vln. & orch.
43. "Arminius," oratorio.
44. Concerto, vln. & orch., in D minor.
45. "Das Lied von der Glocke," soli, choir, and orch.
46. Scottish Fantasia, vln. & orch.
47. "Kol Nidrei," vcello. & orch.
48. 4 Male choruses.
49. 7 Songs.
50. "Achilleus," soli, choir and orch.
51. Symphony in E.
52. "Das Feuerkreuz," soli, choir, & orch.
53.
54. Songs.
55. Canzone, vcello. & orch.
58. Concerto, vln. & orch., D minor.
59. 5 Songs.
60. 9 Choruses.
61. "Ave Maria," vcello. & orch.
62. "Gruss an die heilige Nacht," alto solo, choir, & orch.
63. Swedish Dances, vln. & pf.
64. Scottish Fantasia, vln., harp, & orch.

MAX BRUCH

Without opus-numbers:—

2 Male choruses, " Auf die bei Thermopylæ Gefallen," and " Schlachtgesang des Tyrtäos.
Hebräische Gesänge.
Wettspiele for orch.

KARL GOLDMARK

It has happened over and over again in the history of art that one personality of strong and dominating nature has repressed, instead of stimulating, the productivity of its contemporaries in the same sphere of production, and, instead of founding a school, has to all intents and purposes exhausted the stream of invention which, diverted into other channels, might have fertilised the talents of many perhaps inferior artists. Such a personality was Wagner's, and a marked result of his career and of the change gradually worked by his innovations on all the most important German stages, was that German opera, apart from his works, has been represented, since his influence began to be felt, by strangely few works that can be called "epoch-making." Another inevitable result of such a revolution as came about by Wagner's means is that for a time every contribution to dramatic music, unless it proceeded on purely conventional lines, was considered as a mere reflection of the great master's influence. For the time being, opera seems almost to have quitted Germany for its old home; the long series of German masterpieces in this kind seems to have come to an end, just at the point of time when the Italian schools started into fresh vigour. It is beyond question that among living operatic composers of Germany, none holds or deserves a higher place than the writer whose name stands at the head of this chapter. Yet he has not been able to escape the charge of imitating, more or less consciously, the works and methods of the great dramatic reformer of the nineteenth century, though I venture to predict that the charge will appear less and less well-founded as time goes on. For the same accusation has been brought against very nearly every important opera produced since Wagner's music first became known, and though at first the remark is apt to pass for sapient criticism, in after years it seems hardly credible that it can have been made. Who, for instance, would in the present day accuse Bizet's "Carmen" of owing anything to Wagner? Yet the French critics were considered to have said

KARL GOLDMARK

the last word concerning it when they had asserted that it was influenced by Wagner, and a truer view was long in obtaining acceptance in the composer's own country, though the rest of Europe recognised the work as an original masterpiece. Certain musical critics, and those not of one country alone, seem long in learning that an opera may be constructed on genuinely dramatic lines, with continuous action, richly-coloured orchestration, and definite "individualisation" of its characters, and yet be something more than a mere copy of the man who insisted most strongly on these features, and illustrated them most successfully in his own achievements.

KARL GOLDMARK was born at Keszthely-am-Plattensee, a small town in Hungary, on May 18, 1832; the needy circumstances of his father, a "cantor" in the Jewish synagogue, and the unimportant character of the town in which he lived, precluded him from such opportunities of musical education as have been granted to most composers. Yet a certain amount of music is inherent in the race, and, like many another Jew, young Goldmark made his own opportunities, and did the best he could to cultivate the talent of whose presence he was early conscious. One is reminded of the young Siegfried when one reads of his making little flutes from sticks cut from the hedges; later on he got a violin by some means or other, and the village schoolmaster happily knew enough to start him in the rudiments, with the result that he became, in 1842, advanced enough to enter a small music-school attached to the "Oedenburger Musik-verein," where his talent, first exhibited publicly at a concert given by the society in the winter of 1843-4, manifested itself to such an extent that his parents determined to let him be a musician, and, to that end, managed to send him to Vienna, where for a year (1844-5) he studied under Jansa, a violinist whose fame, to Englishmen of the present generation, rests upon that of his distinguished pupil Lady Hallé, notwithstanding the fact that he himself appeared in London with much success in earlier years. In 1847 he entered the Vienna Conservatorium, becoming a pupil of Böhm for violin, and of Preyer for harmony. Unluckily the institution had to close its doors on account of the revolution of March 1848, and the same crisis in public affairs threw Goldmark on his own resources. He proceeded not only to study every orchestral instrument, as if he had already some presentiment that he was to be a composer, but to obtain an engagement in the orchestra of the theatre at Raab, where his career very nearly came to an abrupt termination, since he was actually led out to be shot on the capitulation of that place to the Government forces. Fortunately for himself and for art, an old friend turned up in the nick of time, and gave satisfactory assurances that the young musician was not, as had been supposed, a rebel, and his life was spared.

He worked hard at composition both before and after his return to Vienna in 1850, when he was befriended to some purpose by a Herr Mittrich, under whose guidance he made a close acquaintance with the great classics of music. About 1854 he was carried away by the Mendelssohn fever, with the intensity of which racial instinct may have had something to do. Of the numerous essays he made in imitation of Mendelssohn, there were enough that were presentable in one kind or another to make it worth while for Goldmark to give a concert consisting of his own works in 1857, and in the same year to give up orchestral playing for good, though he had obtained an engagement at the Karltheater shortly before. A pianoforte quartet, a psalm for solo voices, choir and orchestra, as well as an overture, were brought forward, and the concert was a great success, although Goldmark's name was hardly known at all to the Viennese public. Encouraged by this cordial reception, he was now fully purposed to proceed further in the knowledge of his art as well as of things outside it. He betook himself to Pesth, where he devoted himself to the study, not only of counterpoint and composition, but of languages, literature, and philosophy. Among the great masters whose works he studied most deeply were Bach, Beethoven and Schumann, who have remained the special objects of his admiration through life; but a more definite effect was made upon him, as has been the case with many a young musician, by the study of the score of "Lohengrin," which quite completed the cure of his Mendelssohn-worship. Some of the best of Goldmark's non-theatrical works date from about this time, among them the picturesque overtures, "Sakuntala" and "Penthesilea," the popular symphony known as "Die ländliche Hochzeit" (The Country Wedding), and the first Suite for violin and piano.

In 1859 he gave a concert of his own works at Pesth, and in the following year returned for good to Vienna, where his compositions now began to make their way. The year is marked for the composer as the point at which other people began to play his works. ("Von da ab spielten die Andern meine Sachen," as he says, with a naïve modesty that is very characteristic.) It was the beautiful string quartet in B flat, published as op. 8, and written in Vienna, that particularly delighted Hellmesberger and drew from him a promise of performing all that the composer should produce in the department of chamber-music. The day after the performance of this quartet Goldmark received a visit from Peter Cornelius and Carl Tausig in his dingy lodging, a visit which he regards as the first legitimate triumph of his life. The three were united by a common admiration for Wagner's music, and during the years that followed, Goldmark was not only a successful pianoforte teacher (a sufficiently remarkable fact, considering that until he was fifteen he is said never even to have seen a piano), but was busy with musical criticism. As critic of the *Konstitutionnelle Zeitung* he dared to express himself in favour of Wagner when that master gave a concert in Vienna, concerning which the large majority of journalists took an opportunity of "letting fly" at his music. Goldmark did what he could in the way of pressing upon his readers the necessity of properly producing Wagner's works in Vienna, and we may be sure that he would speak with no lack of enthusiasm. For since his feeling for dramatic music was first awakened by a play for which Kreutzer had written incidental music, and of which a performance was given at the Oedenburg theatre when Goldmark was twelve years old, he had been passionately fond of the stage and operatic music. The old-fashioned "Schweizerfamilie" of Weigl sufficed to send him into a perfect fever of delight when he was a little older, and during his engagement at Raab, Verdi was his musical idol. Thus he was ready to receive the new gospel according to Wagner, and to help the movement forward with all his power. He was not the less ardent a Wagnerian because he refused to become a member of the "Wagner Verein" when it was regularly started, although he himself had been among its original promoters. Whether his refusal, or retirement from membership, arose from a feeling that it was not well for him to pose as a champion of Wagnerism, now that such championship seemed less necessary than it had been, or whether it was, as has been asserted, simply due to pique at his name having been entered on a list of members without his knowledge or consent, does not greatly matter; for there can be no doubt of his complete acceptance of Wagner's theories of dramatic composition, and if there were at first any such doubt, it must have been set at rest when the first of his operas was brought out.

A meeting between Goldmark and Wagner, possibly the only one that took place, is described by a friend of both composers, in the Vienna *Fremdenblatt*, shortly after the production of "Merlin" in November 1886. The writer says: "I was one evening walking with Wagner from Pensing, where he was then staying, to Hacking. He complained bitterly that a chorus in the second act of "Lohengrin" had been taken too fast at a recent performance, and as we walked along he sang the whole number in the correct tempo. As he did not 'hum,' but sang out lustily, the passers-by gave him a wide berth, thinking him tipsy. One man in particular who got out of his way I recognised as Goldmark, walking along reading as he went. I called to him, and introduced him to Wagner, who had never even heard his name. We all returned to Wagner's dwelling, where he complained all the time of his poverty and of his other unhappy circumstances. Goldmark was much moved, and remarked: 'But, Meister, are you not satisfied with the knowledge that your name will be immortal?' This made Wagner very angry, and he replied: 'Never speak to me thus. People consoled Cherubini, as he lay on his deathbed, with hopes of "immortality." He cried "Immortality? Please don't make any bad jokes at such a moment."'"

There are not many instances of first operas making or deserving such success as was achieved by "Die Königin von Saba"; but the absence of early attempts at operatic writing was more than compensated by the extraordinary pains that the composer took over his work. From first to last, no less than seven years were occupied in its preparation; during this time, of course, the composer continued his critical work, as well as his teaching. This last he gave up in the winter season, in order to have more time for his opera. Meyerbeer himself can hardly have done more in the way of writing and re-writing than Goldmark did; the whole of the third act was composed twice over, and many other portions underwent thorough revision. Work of this kind has seldom been more richly rewarded, for from the date of its production at the Court Theatre of Vienna, March 10, 1875, its success has never waned in Germany, while it has been most favourably received in many foreign countries. The composer has personally superintended the getting-up of his work in the chief musical centres of Italy, such as Rome, Milan, Turin, and Bologna, and it has been given in Madrid, St. Petersburg, Warsaw, New York, etc. It is among the works most frequently given in the theatre of its first performance, and at Pesth it has celebrated its 150th night. The cast of the original performance was as follows:—Sulamith, Wilt; Queen, Materna; Astaroth, Siegstädt; Assad, Walter; Solomon, Beck; and High Priest, Rokitansky. Gericke was the conductor.

A "Frühlingshymne" for alto solo, chorus, and orchestra had been brought forward in the previous year; it was then laid aside, to appear, only two years ago, with a new finale written for the occasion. As a natural result of the success of his opera, Goldmark's previous compositions now found wide acceptance; many of the chamber works were only now published, and among the new productions of the composer in this branch of music are a violin concerto in A minor, op. 28, a quintet and trio for piano and strings (ops. 30 and 33), beside numerous songs and piano pieces. It was not for want of opportunity that so long an interval elapsed between the first and second operas; the composer's friends and the various theatrical directors represented to him that he ought not to let the success of "The Queen of Sheba" "get cold" for want of a second work. Goldmark, however, remained firm to his principles of working slowly and not forcing his inspiration. The testimony to this may be trusted, for it comes from a quarter that is far from friendly to Goldmark or his music, viz., the eminent Viennese critic, Dr. Hanslick. The passage occurs in his review of "Merlin," a work in which he could not be expected to find much to admire.

It was in the summer of 1882 that Siegfried Lippiner offered Goldmark the libretto of "Merlin" and for the next four years he devoted himself entirely to its composition, retiring altogether from the world at Gmünden. In a highly-wrought "interview" in a Viennese paper, from which I have already quoted, a story is told of Goldmark's troubles while writing "Merlin," in consequence of the obstreperous singing of some goldfinches in the woods near his windows. These birds resisted every means adopted for their removal, and finally, when one pair were shot by a friend of the distracted musician, another took their place. At last he obtained repose by cutting off the bough in which their nest had been built, and was then able to complete the opera, which was produced in Vienna on November 19, 1886. The cast was as follows:— Viviane, Materna; Merlin, Winkelmann; Demon, Reichenberg; King Arthur, Sommer.

In spite of the favourable reception of the new work, the composer was not satisfied until he had completely re-written the third act; the wisdom of this proceeding was justified by the far greater success attained by the newer version.

The enthusiastic writer in the *Fremdenblatt* is eloquent in his description of the composer's appearance in 1886, as an old-looking man with "flowing locks powdered with silver dust," and a moustache "approaching the autumnal." He is represented as sitting in an armchair, gazing upon a photograph of Schumann, at the top of a house in a by-street in Vienna. He has not spent all his time since "Merlin" was brought out in such contemplations, for numerous and important are the works produced since that time. A second symphony, in E flat, op. 35; the overtures, "Im Frühling" and "Prometheus Bound" (opp. 36 and 38); a violoncello sonata, op. 39, and a second suite for violin and piano, op. 43, have seen the light within the last few years; and his latest work, an overture called "Sappho," was played towards the end of last year at a Philharmonic Concert in Vienna under Richter. It is considered to be the most difficult work yet written for orchestra; this may readily be believed since its key is G flat.

In London, where Goldmark's chamber and orchestral compositions are not infrequently played, it is at least likely that his operas might catch the public ear; they should attract the attention of a manager whose stage management is his strong point, for both are spectacular in a marked degree. In addition to this, they are confessedly the composer's *chef-d'œuvres*, and it is hardly possible for the English public to realise the position among German musicians held by Goldmark until these are brought forward. To the first there attaches the grave objection that it is founded, to some extent, upon a Biblical subject; but the second opera would certainly pass the censorship. With many men an opera is included in their list of compositions, or it may be they have written more than one work for the stage without being regarded chiefly as operatic writers; thus, to take two prominent instances, both Beethoven and Schumann hold their positions in the history of art almost without reference to the single opera which each wrote. Goldmark's two operas, however, represent so large a period of his life and are in all respects so important that his claim to be considered one of the masters of contemporary music rests mainly on them. A story is current that Goldmark, after some casual conversation with a lady to whom he was a stranger, announced himself as "the composer of 'The Queen of Sheba.'" "Dear me!" was the lady's comment; "that must be a very lucrative post!"

The plot of "The Queen of Sheba" is entirely different from that of Gounod's fine opera, but it is certainly not less suitable for operatic purposes. The personages are well contrasted with each other, and the action is continuous and fairly concise. At the opening of the piece we learn that Sulamith, the daughter of the High Priest, is to wed Assad on his return from a martial expedition; the Jewish "local colour" is not long in making its appearance, in an extremely pretty chorus for female voices, with solo for the bride, "Dein Freund ist dein," a passage of unmistakable Hebrew flavour, finely treated. The quiet, dignified music allotted to Solomon is another feature of the whole work, which soon is brought forward; the king finds out from Assad that his affections have been diverted from Sulamith by the sight of a beautiful woman, whom the audience is not long in discovering to be the Queen of Sheba herself, on her way to Jerusalem. The march and chorus which accompany the entrance of the queen are most effective, and the fine piece of six-part writing at the words "Sonne des Mittags" shows the hand of a most accomplished musician. The dramatic climax of the act is the frantic appeal of the infatuated Assad to the queen, and her not unnatural repudiation of the acquaintance. (It is made clear that love-passages have taken place between them.) It was hardly possible that the second act, a romantic scene with an impassioned love-duet for Assad and the queen, should not suggest, in its dramatic structure at least, the famous second act of "Tristan und Isolde," and the difficulty is increased by an episode in which an attendant, after the manner of Brangäne, sings a long *melisma* behind the scenes. If the music is honestly examined, I do not think that the resemblance will be found to be more than a superficial one, and for a great part of it the librettist is alone responsible. The orchestral "Morgendämmerung" with the choral prayer ends the scene suitably, and leads effectively to the second scene of the act, in the interior of the Temple. There is, of course, any amount of Hebrew colouring here, and very well is it managed. It is not quite clear, perhaps, why the queen should be introduced into this scene, in which the marriage of Assad and Sulamith is to take place; but her presence gives fine opportunities for *ensemble* numbers, and a really dramatic climax occurs at the point where Assad, after the High Priest thinks he succeeded in exorcising the evil spirit that is supposed to have caused unfaithfulness, is brought back to the queen's side by a single word from her lips. He is condemned to death, and the sentence is ultimately commuted, at the urgent request of the queen, to banishment in the desert. The well-written duet between Solomon and the queen is preceded by an elaborate ballet, including a very graceful "Almeentanz"; it is followed by a picturesque lament sung by Sulamith and her maidens. In the fourth act, which takes place in the desert, Assad declines the queen's endearments, now lavished upon him; when her wiles are in vain, she leaves him just before a sand-storm comes on, which, after the convenient fashion of operatic cataclysms of all kinds, is enough to give Assad his death, while it leaves entirely unharmed not only the queen, who has just left the stage, but Sulamith, who arrives in time to receive her fickle lover's last breath. The resumption of the pretty *ensemble* "Dein Freund ist dein" from the first act closes the work with a considerable amount of pathos.

The episode of the sand-storm savours a good deal more strongly of the old fashioned opera than of Wagner; one is reminded of the finales of "L'Africaine" and "Aïda" by the amount of imagination that has to be exercised by the audience, for even with the elaborate *mise-en-scène* of Vienna it is quite impossible to divine from the action alone the cause of Assad's death, just as it is difficult to tell why Aïda and Radames, after singing a duet, should expire from asphyxiation in a position in which they are evidently able to breathe the air of the entire theatre. If the richly coloured orchestration, the dexterous manipulation of the numerous large *ensemble* numbers, and occasionally the manner of handling, remind us more or less of the Wagner of the "Lohengrin" period, there are also many characteristics in common with Meyerbeer's work, and the rapid succession of situations obviously intended rather to impress the public than to carry the dramatic truth of the work to the furthest possible point, suggests the manner of the great Jewish opera-maker. Still, with all its superficial brilliancy, its marches and pageants of various kinds, it cannot be denied that the characters are well individualised, or that each stands out from the rest as a real dramatic creation. The calm and dignified strains allotted to Solomon have been alluded to before; they fit the character of the wisest of men as well as the impetuous phrases of the title-part suit the savage and unscrupulous queen, or the gentle accents of Sulamith the Jewish maiden always ready to forgive her lover's aberrations.

It is a pity that the Biblical source of the

subject makes it at present impossible to hope for a performance of this work in England, and it is fortunate that no such objection exists in the case of Goldmark's other opera, the action of which passes in Britain. Founded on a "mystery" by Immermann, "Merlin" has only the most distant connection with the "Morte d'Arthure," from which, of course, it is ultimately derived. From the point of view of the superficial observer, and considering the wide-spread impressions that Goldmark is nothing but a copyist of Wagner, it was, perhaps, a pity that Herr Lippiner knew his Wagner so well as he must have done. Mme. Materna, too, had to create in Viviane a character that could hardly fail to bring back remembrances of precisely the two parts in which the artist is at her best, the Brünnhilde of "Die Walküre," and Kundry in "Parsifal," so that the personality of the singer could not but give colour to the idea, and in some measure affect the success of the work, in spite of her admirable impersonation of the heroine. In a sense, Goldmark had followed Wagner, for the dramatic method of "Merlin" shows as much advance upon that of "The Queen of Sheba" as the style of "Parsifal" does on that of "Lohengrin." The living composer is

KARL GOLDMARK

clearly cognisant of the innovations of his predecessor, and adopts them unhesitatingly; the musical ideas are, however, entirely his own; he has merely chosen to cast them in forms that are of recent origin, rather than in those of older fashion. If in his adoption of the new dramatic methods he exhibits less divergence from the actual style of Wagner than is shown in the two masterpieces of Verdi's old age, it must be remembered that Verdi is of a different nation from the master who first practised, if he did not actually invent, these methods, while Goldmark is of the same nationality. In both his operas certain characteristics appear which seem typical of the Jewish race; the "local colour" of the earlier work is, of course, suggested by its subject, and though this is absent in the later, there are other characteristics generally recognised as Semitic, such as the instinct for brilliant effects on the stage and certain turns of harmony. By these, if by nothing else, Goldmark is differentiated from Wagner, in spite of the fact that in Goldmark's second opera the *leit-motiv* is far more freely used than in his first.

The harp-phrase in triple time which is soon divined as the instrumental equivalent of

Merlin, is accounted for by the magic harp possessed by the seer, which will only sound as long as his moral purity remains. At the loss of this, too, his prophetic power must disappear. The scenario opens in Arthur's "burg," whither Lancelot comes to know from Merlin how the approaching battle with the Saxons will go, and to entreat his aid against the enemy. Merlin calls up a familiar spirit and commands him to use his power in Arthur's favour. The condition of this demon is somewhat pitiable, for he is in Merlin's power, and is constantly compelled to do good actions against his will. It is he who devises a method of depriving Merlin of his skill by ensnaring him in the toils of Viviane's charms. A very effective invocation of Fata Morgana, who plays a part similar to that of Erda in the Wagnerian trilogy, follows, and her prophetic utterances give place, none too soon, to the music which ushers in the victorious Arthur and his knights. Merlin detects in Bedwyr, one of the knights, the signs of treachery, and compels him to confess that he has indeed been plotting against the king. A song of welcome to Arthur is then sung by Merlin, who breaks off suddenly as Viviane's voice is heard singing a wild hunting-song with

FACSIMILE OF AUTOGRAPH SCORE BY CARL GOLDMARK

a family resemblance to the Walküre cry. A fine ensemble with seven solo parts now leads up to a scene in which Viviane, asked to crown the singer, touches him for that purpose, when it turns out that her mere touch, although he shrinks from it, has made his harp useless in his hand. His attempts to strike its chords are entirely ineffectual; and, throwing the crown at Merlin's feet, Viviane runs off, and Arthur himself puts the wreath on Merlin's head as the act closes. The incident of the harp suddenly made silent is one of those things which, in themselves suggestive enough, can scarcely ever make much effect upon the stage; even the best artists rarely attain to such perfection of gesture as to deceive the audience into thinking that the "property" harps they pretend to play are really sounding, and the sight of a singer vigorously twanging a harp without the slightest audible result is only too common a spectacle in "Tannhäuser" and other operas where the instrument in the orchestra has to supply the sounds supposed to come from the instrument in the singer's hand. The effect of the passage, therefore, unless the work is very carefully managed, must almost certainly be to create an idea that the harp-player in the band has forgotten his cue, or else that the representative of Merlin has made the gesture of playing the harp too soon.

The matter-of-fact part of the next act is got over with a laudable brevity. Modred and Bedwyr conspire against Arthur, rather unwisely choosing Merlin's magic garden for their conversation; the king comes to the same place afterwards to take leave of Merlin before going to battle, and announces that the kingdom is to be left in Modred's hands until his return. This is resented by Lancelot, who in good set terms accuses Modred of treachery, with the usual result that Merlin's superhuman knowledge of character is called upon to pronounce on Modred's honesty. His momentary yielding to temptation at the sight of Viviane has deprived him of this faculty as well as of his proficiency on the harp, for he declares Modred to be innocent. Between this false decision and the demonstration of its falsity when Modred's revolt actually breaks out, there comes a scene full of musical possibilities, in which Viviane, led in by the Demon, is induced to invoke, by means of a magic veil, all kinds of spirits, who dance according to the accepted traditions of the habits of their kind. Merlin, entering, warns

Viviane that the veil, if wrapped round her head, will hold her fast; she, of course, uses the information for her own purposes, enveloping Merlin in the veil at a point when he tries to break free from her endearments. In spite of all this, the love of the two is represented as being a real and deep emotion that is capable of baffling the fiend at the end. The veil changes to a magic chain confining Merlin, and the magic garden is at the same moment transformed into a dreary waste. No very obvious dramatic purpose is served by this last change, such as that which accounts for the fading of Klingsor's magic garden in "Parsifal" —an incident which cannot have been unknown to Goldmark's librettist. The state of the garden continues into the third act, in the early part of which occurs an effective scene for Morgana, a graceful chorus of Viviane's handmaidens, and another of mocking spirits rejoicing in Merlin's discomfiture. All in vain news is brought of Arthur's perilous position in the battle; Merlin cannot free himself by his own power. Like Vanderdecken, he proposes to barter his eternal happiness for present freedom from the chain; the demon appears, agrees to the bargain, and at once he is free, and the garden is in its former luxuriance. Merlin goes forth to fight, and during his absence a scene of remarkable effectiveness passes between Viviane and her attendants, at the close of which, as she approaches the climax of her song of triumph to the victorious Merlin, mournful strains are heard, and the seer is borne in wounded to death. A stately death-march gains immensely in effect, of course, from the brilliant music that has preceded it. As the lovers are saying their last farewells, the demon appears to claim his part of the bargain; but Viviane, recalling the prophetic words of Morgana, and possibly, too, the finale of "Der fliegende Holländer," stabs herself, an action which has the usual operatic result of driving off the disappointed fiend, and reuniting the lovers in a better world.

The work is orchestrated with enormous ability and feeling for colour; the harmonic progressions are sometimes daring, but never indefensible on technical grounds, although a certain section of the German press found grievous fault in this particular. Another favourite charge to bring against "Merlin" was the alleged lack of human interest, and the prominence of the magic and diabolic elements in the story. This last was a useful accusation both for the anti-Wagnerians, who shook their heads over the composer's "modern" tendencies, and for the Wagnerians, who, of course, did not wish to accept too heartily a man that was no longer to be counted among the professed members of the party. There is no doubt that demons, fairies, and such like personages have gone a little out of fashion in opera of late years; the magic element, once almost a matter of course in German opera, if nowhere else, was used with the utmost restraint by Wagner, and has entirely or almost entirely disappeared in the works of the newest Italian school. Yet there is no reason why this should be so; opera at the best of times is a purely conventional form of art, and objections that are valid enough with regard to plays do not hold good in regard to the musical drama. To enumerate the successful operas in which there is a spice of the supernatural would take far too long, and when we remember that the most popular opera in existence at the present moment, Gounod's "Faust," relies on its supernatural part for all its effect, it seems scarcely enough to build a condemnation upon, that a new work deals with such factors. Zamiel has had his day, perhaps —more's the pity!—but Mephistopheles still flourishes, and he and his kind seem likely to hold the stage for many years to come. The fault seems to me to lie rather on the other side; and in "Merlin," I cannot help thinking that either the librettist or the composer has erred in treating the figures of Merlin and Viviane as if they had any real existence. The wrong note is struck, not by the supernatural power of the one, or the mysterious witcheries of the other, but by the sentimental, quasi-religious ending. The union of these lovers, begun as a device of the demon to ruin Merlin, ends as it were in the odour of sanctity and with the blessings of the audience, if not exactly of the Church. The truth is that the interesting figures of the action are one and all a little removed from ordinary human experience: Arthur is not nearly as finished a portrait as the Solomon of the earlier opera, Lancelot and the other knights are little more than "supers," and the interest is concentrated on Merlin and Viviane, with Fata Morgana and the Demon for subordinate characters. This being so—and it is difficult to see how it could be otherwise—the attempt should have been made to carry the thing off without reference to "human interest" at all—to make us feel that the atmosphere of the whole was of a purely imaginary world, and to keep all psychology and sentimental speculations as to the future as far as possible from the minds of the audience. The intensely human interest which Wagner managed to put into such extra-human figures as Kundry is not within the power of less highly gifted men to reach, and the Bayreuth master knew the secret of surrounding his mythical heroine with more or less ordinary human beings, and of showing her in relation to these.

The changes in the third act, made since the publication of the piano score, have certainly improved the real effect of the end. From the close of Viviane's song of triumph the action now proceeds as follows:—The battle is actually fought on the stage, for a short space, during which Merlin kills Modred in single combat; the Demon relates the subsequent course of the fight to Viviane, and tells her that it was he who freed the seer from his chain. Morgana passes across the stage at the back, reminding Viviane of her vision, and soon after the wounded Merlin is brought in as in the earlier version. The work now closes with the funeral march far more impressively and suitably than before. It may not bear that minute analysis into which one is tempted by its resemblance to Wagner's works, but from the ordinary operatic standpoint there can be no doubt as to the brilliancy and effectiveness of Goldmark's second opera.

It is to be hoped that he will in time add a third stage-work to these already existing, for herein lies his power, rather than in the domain of absolute music. His achievements in this latter department—taking the term "absolute" in its widest sense of "non-dramatic" music—are by no means to be despised. His best productions, apart from the theatre, are perhaps those which rank as "programme-music." The symphony called "The Country Wedding" has a most agreeable pastoral flavour, and indeed the only reproach that can be brought against it is in respect of its form. The first of its five movements is a set of variations on a rustic march, the theme of which is given out, quaintly enough, by violoncellos and double-basses alone. In spite of the interest and variety of the variations, it is difficult for those who regard the orthodox "first movement" form as one of permanent value and beauty, to forgive its absence in a work calling itself a symphony. For these critics, however, it is easy to call the work a "suite," in order to satisfy their consciences and enjoy the music at the same time. The second movement, called "Brautlied," is a naïve and expressive, sometimes almost plaintive, little section, and the succeeding scherzo, called "serenade," is scored with great delicacy and originality. It was rather a bold expedient to write the movement in D, when the symphony is in E flat, but the gain in brightness is undeniable, and the fourth movement leads back to the principal key by way of G minor. This, called, for no very evident reason, "Im Garten," is remarkable for a curious cadenza in the string parts at the reprise. The finale, inscribed "Tanz," is a very effective section, and in its course the subject of the preceding movement is brought in again, as if the bridal pair took a walk in the garden between the dances. The second symphony, in the same key as the first, has a good deal of the same rustic character, though it is written to no "programme." It cries aloud for scenery and action, for it is far more operatically than symphonically conceived. The curious want of refinement in the trumpet-tune played as the trio of the scherzo is, happily, not a very common characteristic of the composer.

The "Sakuntala" overture is a fine piece of colouring in the Oriental style; the admirable cleverness of its orchestration may be held to make up for what it lacks in interest of themes or development. The "Penthesilea" overture is a picturesque and vivid presentment of the Amazon queen, needing no words for its elucidation. The vigorous main section in G allegro is interrupted by a graceful andante in the same triple time, but in E, and the close of the work is very striking: after a slight pause, a full chord of E major is given out by the wind-instruments, and answered by the chord of C in the strings passing into E; again the chord of A in the wind is followed by that of F; F passing in like manner into A in the strings, and painting for us most unmistakably the death-blow given by Achilles. The short coda, built on new material, is decidedly impressive.

The first of the suites for violin and piano is divided into five movements, and is throughout interesting and well-written for both instruments. The second, if not quite so attractive, gives many good opportunities to a skilful violinist, and its success in the hands of an artist like Señor Sarasate, for whom it was written, is undeniable. Recently the composer has to a great extent given up the larger forms of chamber music—a matter of regret, for in the works of his early time in this branch of composition he achieved some noteworthy results in the way of colour. It is indeed as a musical colourist that Goldmark's name will endure; whether he handles voices or instruments, and whether in larger or smaller groups, he is nearly always successful in getting the precise shade of colouring that is desirable. His arrangements of material generally arrest attention and keep it fixed, and this mainly by the disposition of the forces at his command. He is a master of superficial effect, though his actual inventive power is not exceptionally great, by any means. His melodies have neither the grandeur of Wagner's ideas nor the flowing grace and freedom of Bruch's, and the task of transforming or developing themes appears to be merely a task to him, and to possess no such attractions as the greatest composers, whether living or dead, have found in it. Still, as the best writer for the stage working in Germany, he has a distinguished place of his own among contemporary musicians.

CATALOGUE OF PUBLISHED COMPOSITIONS BY KARL GOLDMARK.

Op.
1.
2.
3.
4. Trio, pf. & strings.
5. "Sturm und Drang," 9 pf. pieces.
6.
7.
8. String quartet in B flat.
9. String quintet in A minor.
10. "Regenlied" for choir.
11. Suite, pf. & vln., in E.
12. 3 Pf. pieces, 4 hands.
13. Overture, "Sakuntala."
14. 2 Male choruses.
15. "Frühlingsnetz," male quartet, 4 horns and pf.
16. "Meeresstille und Glückliche Fahrt," male voices and horns.
17. 2 Male choruses.
18. 12 Songs.
19. Scherzo, orch.
20. "Beschwörung," song.
21. 4 Songs.
22. Dances, orch.
23. "Frühlingshymne," alto solo, choir, and orch.
24. "Im Fuscherthal," 6 songs for choir.
25. Sonata, vln. & pf.
26. Symphony, "Die ländliche Hochzeit."
27. "Die Königin von Saba," grand opera in 4 acts.

KARL GOLDMARK

Op.
28. Concerto, vln. & orch., in A minor.
29. "Novelletten," preludes & fugues, pf.
30. Quintet, pf. & strings, B flat.
31. Overture, "Penthesilea."
32. Songs.
33. Trio, pf. & strings.
34. 4 Songs.
35. Symphony, E flat.
36. Overture, "Im Frühling."
37. 8 Songs.
38. Overture, "Prometheus Bound."
39. Sonata, pf. & vcello.
40. ⎫
41. ⎬ as yet unpublished.
42. ⎭
43. Suite, vln. & pf.

Without opus-number:—"Merlin," grand opera in 3 acts.
Overture, "Sappho."

JOSEF RHEINBERGER

OF the many classes of musical material, none was more prolific of influence upon German composers of the earlier generations than the organ. The art of organ-composition and performance (the two were so constantly joined in one individual that they are fitly spoken of together), starting in Italy and the Netherlands almost simultaneously, found in Germany a soil prepared for their growth by the Lutheran institution of chorales. For the fact that these hymns were in some sense a protest against the elaborate polyphonic music of the Roman Church tended to discourage the development of the more intricate vocal forms, while the simplicity of the tunes required much of the musical interest to be transferred to the instruments which supported and accompanied them. The long pauses which, for very practical reasons, were made between the lines, gave an obvious opportunity to a clever organist to improvise "interludes" of greater or less elaboration; and we know what such interludes ultimately became in the hands of Sebastian Bach, many of whose sublimest compositions are little more than a development of the plan which still subsists in the Lutheran Church. After Bach the "royal line" of composers, as it may be called, gave up the organ as the central root of music, and with the rise of the classical orchestra the greatest productions of Germany ceased gradually to be influenced as strongly as they had been by the king of instruments. There has not failed a line of organists *par excellence* in Germany, but few of these have attained so high a level of distinction, whether as a composer for this instrument or in other departments of art, as JOSEF RHEINBERGER, who, now that Merkel is dead, may be regarded as the chief representative in modern music of the Pachelbels and Buxtehudes of the older day. In the long list of his works it is very curious to see the very large proportion of the compositions in which the organ plays an important if not the only part.

Rheinberger's birthplace is a sort of earthly paradise among deep forests, with lovely views of the upper Rhine valley. Vaduz, a small town four miles from the lake of Constance, used to be the capital of the smallest of the German Confederations. Here the fourth son of Prince Liechtenstein's treasurer (Rentmeier), Peter Rheinberger was born on March 17, 1839, and baptised in the historical church of St. Florian by the names of Josef Gabriel. Neither of the parents was musical to any appreciable extent, though his father was keen enough to wish for, and at length to obtain, a new organ for the parish church, little suspecting that the first organist appointed to it would be his youngest son. Frau Rheinberger's brother, a priest of a village in the neighbourhood, persuaded her to allow the village schoolmaster to give her daughters lessons in the guitar and singing. To these lessons the little four-year-old brother used to listen by stealth, and it was noticed that he profited by what he heard, for he was learning faster than his sisters. The father was wise enough to let him learn the pianoforte, at first on an old harpsichord belonging to the schoolmaster, and afterwards on a real piano got for the purpose from Vienna. For two years he worked assiduously, and soon became an excellent reader of music. He was now introduced to the study of musical theory by one Sebastian Pöhly, a pensioned schoolmaster in Schlanders, who, knowing that an organist would soon be required for Vaduz, undertook to make the child fit for the post. To this end he invented an apparatus by which the organ-pedals could be brought within reach of the little player's feet, and at the age of seven, Josef Rheinberger was actually appointed as the regular organist of the parish church. Within the following year the proud parents "assisted" at a performance of a three-part mass with organ accompaniment composed by their son. Hearing of this wonderful child, the Bishop of Chur, who had a taste for music, invited the father to introduce the boy to him in order that his musical ability might be tested. A " Salve Regina," for four male voices and organ, was put before him on the organ desk, and he was told to play it while the Bishop and the clergy sang. After a few bars this *enfant terrible* turned round and calmly informed the Bishop that he was singing out of tune ! Happily the good-natured dignitary took it in good part and laughingly gave the boy a ducat for his honesty and fearlessness. Another very characteristic story dates from about the same time. There were in the organ-loft at Vaduz a number of masses of which the young organist did not approve; so one day during service he stuffed them all, *à la* Hedda Gabler, into the stove, which was put in the organ-loft for his convenience. His crime was discovered by a terrific volume of smoke arising, which naturally alarmed and disturbed the congregation. He probably had to thank his youth that this *auto da fè* had no serious consequences, or, perhaps, the masses were of such a kind that the authorities were secretly not sorry to be rid of them. Still, one wonders what would have become of an English boy in the same position who should have destroyed even "Jackson in F"!

The elder Rheinberger, though he seems to have lacked any musical talent, was fully conscious of the responsibility of his position as the father of a musical genius, and was careful to protect him from influences concerning which he was not quite sure. For example, when Liszt passed through the neighbourhood on a concert-tour, the boy was not allowed to go and hear him, since the father, or his musical advisers, dreaded the measure of charlatanism which they suspected to exist in the great virtuoso. The circumstance speaks, of course, more eloquently for their artistic conscience than for their worldly wisdom.

At the age of nine Rheinberger heard a string quartet for the first time. The auguries were good, for the quartet was one of Mozart's, and the day was the feast of St. Cecilia. A few dilettanti came over for the day from the neighbouring Austrian town of Feldkirch, bringing their instruments with them. The boy was allowed to turn the leaves for the leader of the quartet, a revenue official (*Cameralbeamter*) named Schrammel, and his delight in the new musical revelation was so great as to attract attention; his casual remark, that the violins sounded a semitone higher than his piano at home, was found after the performance to be accurate, proving him to possess the invaluable sense of musical pitch that is one of the most certain proofs of natural capacity for the art. After some persuasion, Rheinberger's father was induced to allow the boy to go with Herr Schrammel to Feldkirch to be taught music, especially theory, by the choir director there, Philipp Schmutzer. One severe condition was attached to the permission: that the organist's duties at Vaduz were not to be neglected. So

JOSEF RHEINBERGER

for some two years the boy trudged the nine or ten miles between the two places every Saturday and Monday. Besides the regular music-lessons he practised concerted music with the violin every day, since Schrammel was an ardent amateur, and no doubt made the most of his opportunities. His knowledge of other kinds of music grew rapidly from a lucky friendship he formed with a superannuated schoolmaster, who not only possessed copies of Beethoven's sonatas, Bach's "Wohltemperirtes Clavier," and Mozart's operas (it must be remembered that in the days before cheap music had been introduced such a library as this was not often to be found in out-of-the-way towns), but had known Mozart personally. The story is told by a writer in the *Neue Musik-Zeitung*, who gives the following conversation as reported by the old teacher: "I was in 1790 in Vienna as *Schulpräparand*,* and fondly thought I had a lovely bass voice. To train this I was recommended to Kapellmeister Mozart. I went to him, and found a well-dressed, fine gentleman, who received me

---

* A master whose work consists of preparing the pupils at home for their school work.

graciously. I naturally wanted to show off the full power of my voice, and I sang, I suppose, a bit too loud. ['Ein bisl zu laut.'] Mozart jumped up from the piano, stopped his ears, and, laughing, said, 'Excuse me, dear sir, but I can't teach oxen to sing' ['Sie verzeihen's, lieber Herr, aber an Ochsen kann ich's Singen net lehren ']." Beside the music above-mentioned, the old teacher had a cupboard full of music of all kinds, at which Rheinberger cast longing eyes. He was given permission to take out one piece at a time, but on the rather harsh condition that he was to play it, *from memory*, to the teacher before exchanging it for another. No doubt the training did the boy good, and it may be maintained that the strict discipline to which he was subjected in one way or another helped to invigorate his musical constitution, and to deepen the roots of his musical knowledge. If there is one quality for which Rheinberger is pre-eminently distinguished, it is the thoroughness with which all of music that can be taught has been mastered.

Small as Feldkirch was there were many opportunities of hearing music, and even of taking part, and the young Rheinberger appeared several times at concerts. In 1850 he returned home and spent a year in hard study, preparing to enter the Munich Conservatorium. At that institution he remained from October 1851 to 1854, learning the piano from Prof. Emil Leonhard, organ from Prof. Herzog, and counterpoint from J. J. Maier, the famous curator of the musical department of the Munich Library. Professor Niecks states, on good authority, that the last-named musician is regarded by Rheinberger as the master to whom he owed most. On leaving the Conservatorium, Rheinberger became a private pupil of Franz Lachner, and remained in Munich earning money by giving lessons on his own account. On Professor Leonhard's resignation of his post in the Conservatorium, Rheinberger was appointed to succeed him, in 1859, as professor of the pianoforte; this situation he only held a year, for in the next year he was given the more important office of professorship of composition. His op. 1, a set of four piano pieces, was not published until the year of his appointment as teacher, although the pieces had been written three years before. In 1860 he obtained his first appointment as organist in Munich, to the Court church of St. Michael; in 1864 he undertook to conduct the Munich Oratorio Society, whose accompanist he had been since 1854; and about the same time he became "solo-repetitor" (*i.e.*, "maestro al cembalo") to the Hoftheater. The first of these offices was given up in 1866, the second in 1877, and the third in 1867.

It is curious that in the dated list of his compositions there should be none which appears to have originated during his tenure of his first important organist's post, and that he should have produced no works for the organ, a class of composition in which he was afterwards to make so great a success. His long connexion with the choral society bore fruit in the numerous works for choir and orchestra, and his employment at the theatre gave opportunity for the production of two works in the shape of incidental music to Raimund's *Unheilbringende Krone*, and to a version of Calderon's *Magico prodigioso*, the second of which was a great success when given under the composer's direction. An opera, "Die sieben Raben," was not produced until 1869 (May 23), when the composer's connexion with the theatre had been severed.

That this severance was not wholly due to the rapidity with which the Wagnerian influences were gaining ground in the Munich opera just at this time is pretty conclusively proved by the fact that Rheinberger, upon his resignation, accepted the professorship of counterpoint and organ in the new Munich Royal Music School, founded by Von Bülow. Still, there can be no doubt that throughout his career Rheinberger has been a pronounced anti-Wagnerian, and it is very natural that the atmosphere of the theatre should not have been very congenial to him. In 1867, the year of his new appointment, he received the title of Royal Professor, and in the same year he married a Frl. von Hoffnaas, the author of the words of some of his most successful compositions, among others, of "Toggenburg," op. 76, and "Montfort," op. 145, both works of large calibre. She died recently.

When the Hoch Conservatorium at Frankfort was founded the direction was offered to Rheinberger, but declined by him; in 1877 he succeeded Wüllner as Königliche Hofcapellmeister (*i.e.*, director of the Court church music). This new appointment stimulated him to the composition of many ecclesiastical works, and from this time onwards sacred music has taken an ever more prominent place in his list of works. His Masses, to say nothing of the early compositions mentioned above, are eleven in number, and among them are one for a single voice and organ, one for three female voices, and one in eight parts. This last, op. 109, was the immediate cause of his obtaining the order of knighthood of Gregory the Great, from Pope Leo XIII., to whom it was dedicated; another, lately published, op. 172, is for male choir, organ and wind-instruments. Besides these there are two settings of the "Stabat Mater," op. 16 and op. 138; two Requiems, opp. 60 and 84, the former written in honour of those who fell in the war of 1870–71; many sacred part-songs, choruses, and single songs, and no less than sixteen organ sonatas, the latest, op. 175, in G sharp minor, besides other organ pieces. An oratorio, "Christoforus,"* and several cantatas, sacred and secular, for children, as well as a more recent work, "Die Stern von Bethlehem," a Christmas cantata, op. 164, are among his more successful choral works, and a comic opera, in four acts, "Thürmers Töchterlein," op. 70 (produced at Munich, April 23, 1873), is to be added to the dramatic works already mentioned.

* Given first in England by Miss Holland's choir, Feb. 24, 1885.

FACSIMILE OF AUTOGRAPH SCORE BY JOSEF RHEINBERGER

JOSEF RHEINBERGER

Much of his earliest success as a composer was due to his symphony entitled "Wallenstein," which bears the early opus-number 10; it was given under Rheinberger's direction at Munich, Leipzig, and Prague, with great success. Another symphony in F, op. 87, is known as the "Florentine Symphony," since it was commissioned by the Società Orchestrale of Florence. His overture, "Demetrius," is a good example of the happy treatment of national themes.

To English amateurs, the name of Rheinberger suggests at once the quartet in E flat for pianoforte and strings, a work which has been extraordinarily popular in England since a very few years after its composition. In spite of a certain want of distinction in the themes, a defect which is common to many works of the composer, the treatment of the materials is so uniformly skilful, and the instruments are so effectively employed, that the vogue it has enjoyed need surprise no one. Since music for wind-instruments has begun to receive attention in London (owing to the establishment of the Wind Instrument Chamber Music Society), the Nonet, for wind and strings, op. 139, has been performed several times: it is a good example of the composer's complete knowledge of the nature of the various instruments, and indeed it is hard to mention a single work of his which is not perfectly suited to the medium for which it is intended. His pianoforte pieces are models in their kind in this respect. One has only to look at the first bars of "Die Jagd," a piece included in Rheinberger's op. 5, and dating as far back as 1862 or so, to see that he has got the greatest possible effect out of very little : for the piece, though it sounds fairly difficult, is within the powers of very ordinary performers.

In looking through the long list of his works it is curious to see how many of the early compositions have made their mark. The "Wallenstein" symphony is only op. 10; a most effective duo for two pianofortes is op. 15 ; "Aus Italien," a group of pieces containing some of the composer's happiest inspirations, is op. 29 ; and the famous quartet is op. 38. This, taken in connection with the comparative want of general recognition that has befallen many of his later works, seems to indicate that the fountain of his inspiration has not kept its freshness ; and the sign is, perhaps, not wholly misleading. The department of his work in which the highest level has been maintained throughout his career is beyond question that of the organ compositions. The whole series of organ sonatas, covering as they do a period of over twenty years, has a richness of colouring, a mastery of effect, and a constant flow of beautiful ideas that are by no means always found in his other works. If we except the works of Gustav Merkel, these sonatas are by far the most valuable addition to the literature of the instrument since the sonatas of Mendelssohn. In many of his larger works, too, whether for orchestra or voices, there is a freedom of manipulation and a real breadth of treatment that appeal strongly to the musical sense, and successfully veil the occasional thinness, not to say poverty, of invention.

In early life Rheinberger learnt easily all that could be taught, and in later years he has taught successfully all that can be learnt. Those who are the most original and in the highest sense distinguished among composers very rarely attain great success as teachers of the art in which they themselves excel. It often happens that they have assimilated its technicalities so unconsciously that they are unable to impart them to others; and the great creative genius is seldom very tolerant of the difficulties encountered by natures less richly endowed.

Rheinberger has been called, and not without justice, the best teacher of composition since Hauptmann. By the kindness of a pupil of Rheinberger's, Dr. G. J. Bennett, I am able to give a somewhat detailed description of the course of study adopted by him, for composition pupils, who, strangely enough, are never taught separately, but always in classes or smaller groups. The course extends over three years, and each class contains from twelve to twenty-four pupils. The work consists principally of "the composition of fugues, canons, variations, etc., at the blackboard, pupils being called on in turn to go to the blackboard, the whole being supervised, corrected, and often entirely condemned, by Rheinberger. The work is copied into manuscript books by all the pupils, and at the next lesson the master calls on a pupil to play the piece as far as it is done, and it is then continued from that point. The composition of a fully developed fugue, or a set of variations, extends over several lessons. Rheinberger frequently suggests at the piano the manner in which the work should be continued.

"I think that his strong point as a master is his truly wonderful command of free counter-

JOSEF RHEINBERGER

point, combined with modern free harmonic treatment. He does not believe in the practice of strict counterpoint—in fact, he does not teach it at all. In the blackboard work he always insists on some individuality: mere correct, pedantic counterpoint has immediately to be rubbed out. Many of the fugues, canons, or variations written in this way are good and even charming compositions, far above the usual merely correct contrapuntal work done in schools. One set of variations for string quartet so produced has been published by him. Although Rheinberger is an advocate of strict classical forms, and strongly opposed to Wagner's principles, in other respects he is by no means a pedant. In matters of harmony he is extremely free, and in part-writing he continually allows progressions which would horrify many masters, but which are always justifiable by the natural flow of the individual parts. The scheme of teaching for three years is as follows:—

"First year.—Free harmonisation of chorales, including *canto fermo* in alto, tenor, and bass; the same for strings with florid counterpoint, free florid counterpoint in four parts, and rapid review of harmony based on Hauptmann and Richter.

"Second year.—First half of lesson: Double counterpoint, and, later, fugue, vocal and instrumental, in two to six parts; double and triple fugue.—Second half of lesson: Instrumentation, based on Berlioz, comprising a complete description of instruments, their compass, etc., and scoring of movements, usually slow movements from Mozart or Beethoven's sonatas or quartets, for small orchestra.

"Third year.—First half of lesson: Canon, at all intervals, usually with a free bass, and double canon.—Second half of lesson: Choruses on a chorale with free accompaniment for strings; choruses in six, seven, eight parts, unaccompanied, and on a chorale. Composition of free variations for string quartet, and analysis of sonatas and symphonies.

"In instrumentation he holds some very old-fashioned views. He has, for instance, a great objection to reiterated chords for the wind, as in the scherzo of Beethoven's eighth symphony, and in the 'Italian' symphony of Mendelssohn.

"Although he also occupies the position of principal organ-professor at the Musikschule, I think that his organ-lessons are of less value than those in counterpoint and composition.

JOSEF RHEINBERGER

He is a believer in the colourless style of playing so prevalent in Germany. Bach is taken very slowly and with little change of registering, and Rheinberger is entirely out of sympathy with modern French organ-music—in fact, with any music introducing staccato playing on the organ. This is possibly to be accounted for partly by the state of organs in Germany.

"Although his manner is naturally proud and ceremonious, and occasionally harsh when teaching dull or lazy pupils, he is uniformly kind to those who work regularly, and is very much respected by them. He teaches a great number of foreigners, and among these the most talented are frequently Americans: for he enjoys in America an even higher reputation than in England."

It will interest English readers to learn that he was delighted with "The Mikado" when it was given at Munich by a travelling company.

On the other hand he was disappointed with "The Golden Legend," holding Sir Arthur Sullivan's strong point to be the composition of comic music, and discerning, what few othercritics of this work have found, a Wagnerian influence in it. Like other strong opponents of Wagner's methods and theories, he fancies the existence of such influences even among his fellow anti-Wagnerians.

CATALOGUE OF PUBLISHED COMPOSITIONS BY JOSEF RHEINBERGER.

Op.
1. 4 Pieces, pf.
2. 5 Choruses.
3. 7 Songs.
4. 5 Songs.
5. 3 Small pf. pieces.
6. 3 Studies, pf.
7. 3 Pieces, pf.
8. "Waldmärchen," pf.
9. 5 Studies, pf.
10. "Wallenstein," symphony.
11. Pf. pieces.
12. Toccata, pf.
13. "Tarantella," pf., 4 hands.
14. 24 Preludes, pf.
15. Duo, 2 pfs.
16. "Stabat Mater," choir, stringed orch. & organ.
17. 2 Balladen, choir.
18. Overture, "Taming of the Shrew."
19. Toccatina, pf.
20. "Die sieben Raben," romantic opera in 3 acts.

JOSEF RHEINBERGER

Op.
21. "Wasserfee," vocal quartet & pf.
22. 4 Songs.
23. Fantasiestück, pf.
24. 4 Vocal quartets.
25. "Lockung," vocal quartet & pf.
26. 7 Songs.
27. 1st Organ sonata, C minor.
28. 4 Humoresken, pf.
29. "Aus Italien," 3 pf. pieces.
30. 7 Pf. duets (from the music to "Der Wunderthätige Magus").
31. 5 Part-songs.
32. "Jairus's Daughter," cantata for children.
33. Prelude & fugue, pf.
34. Trio, pf. and strings.
35. Hymn for female choir and harp.
36. 9 Duets, pf. (from the music to "Die unheilbringende Krone").
37. "Der arme Heinrich," Singspiel for children.
38. Quartet, pf. & strings, in E flat.
39. 6 Pf. pieces, in fugal form.
40. 5 Motets, choir.
41. 7 Songs.
42. Pf. studies.
43. Capriccio giocoso, pf.
44. 3 Male choruses.
45. 2 Pf. studies on a theme by Handel.
46. "Passionsgesang," choir and organ.
47. Sonata symphonique, pf.
48. 4 Male choruses.
49. 10 Organ trios.

Op.

50. "Das Thal von Espingo," ballad, choir & orch.
51. Improvisation on a theme from "Die Zauberflöte," pf.
52. 5 Part-songs.
53. 3 Klaviervorträge, pf.
54. 4 Hymns, soprano & organ.
55. 8 Songs.
56. 4 Vocal quartets, with strings & pf.
57. 7 Songs.
58. 6 Vocal quartets.
59. Studies, pf.
60. Requiem, choir and orch.
61. Theme & variations, pf.
62. Mass for one voice & organ.
63. 8 Part-songs.
64. "Maitag," 3-part female choruses.
65. 2nd Organ sonata in A flat.
66. 3 Studies, pf.
67. 6 Preludes, pf.
68. 6 Fugal pieces, pf.
69. 3 Sacred part-songs.
70. "Thürmers Töchterlein," comic opera in 4 acts.
71. "König Erich," ballad, vocal quartet & pf.
72. "Aus den Ferientagen," 4 pf. duets.
73. 5 Male choruses.
74. 5 Male choruses.
75. 2 Vocal quartets.
76. "Toggenburg," soli, choir and pf., or orch.
77. Sonata, pf. & vcello., E flat.
78. 3 Pf. pieces.

JOSEF RHEINBERGER

Op.
79. Fantasia, orch. or pf., 4 hands.
80. 5 Part-songs.
81. "Die todte Braut," romance, mezzo soprano, choir, & orch.
82. String quintet in A minor.
83. Missa brevis in D minor.
84. Requiem in E flat.
85. 7 Male choruses.
86. 7 Male quartets.
87. Symphony ("Florentine") in F.
88. 3rd Organ sonata in G.
89. String quartet in C minor.
90. "Vom Rheine," 6 male choruses.
91. "Johannisnacht," male quartet and pf.
92. Sonata, pf. and vcello., in C.
93. Theme and variations, string quartet.
94. Pf. concerto in A flat.
95. 2 Choruses.
96. 3 Latin hymns, for female choir.
97. "Klärchen auf Eberstein," ballad, soli, choir, & orch.
98. 4th Organ sonata in A minor.
99. Pf. sonata in D flat.
100. 7 Male choruses.
101. 3 Vortragsstudien, pf.
102. "Wittekind," ballade, male choir & orch.
103. 3 Vocal duets.
104. Toccata, pf.
105. Sonata, vln. & pf., in E minor.
106. 2 Romantic songs, 4 voices & orch.
107. 5 Hymns for choir.

Op.
- 108. "Am Strom," 6 part-songs.
- 109. Mass in E flat for double choir, ded. to Leo XIII.
- 110. Overture to Schiller's "Demetrius."
- 111. 5th Organ sonata in F sharp.
- 112. 2nd Trio, pf. & strings, in A.
- 113. 6 Studies for pf. (left-hand).
- 114. Quintet, pf. & strings, in C.
- 115. Toccata, pf.
- 116. 4 Male choruses.
- 117. "Missa Sanctissimæ Trinitatis," choir, in F.
- 118. 6 Two-part hymns, with organ.
- 119. 6th Organ sonata, in E flat minor.
- 120. "Christoforus," legend, for soli, choir, & orch.
- 121. Trio, pf. & strings, in B flat.
- 122. Sonata in C minor, pf. 4-hands.
- 123. 24 Fughetten for organ.
- 124. 8 Songs for 4 voices.
- 125. 7 Male choruses.
- 126. Mass, 3-part female choir, in A.
- 127. 7th Organ sonata, in F minor.
- 128. 4 Songs.
- 129. 3 Italian songs.
- 130. 6 Male choruses.
- 131. 6 Female choruses.
- 132. 8th Organ sonata in E minor.
- 133. 4 Motets, 6-part choir.
- 134. Easter hymn, double choir.
- 135. Pf. sonata in E flat.
- 136. 14 Songs.
- 137. Organ concerto in F, with orch.
- 138. Stabat Mater, choir & orch.

JOSEF RHEINBERGER

Op.
- 139. Nonet, wind & strings.
- 140. 5 Hymns, choir & organ.
- 141. 6 Male choruses.
- 142. 9th Organ sonata in B flat minor.
- 143. Ballade, male choir & brass, "Die Rosen von Hildesheim."
- 144. 3 Male choruses.
- 145. "Montfort," soli, choir, & orch.
- 146. 10th Organ sonata, in B minor.
- 147. String quartet in F.
- 148. 11th Organ sonata in D minor.
- 149. Suite, organ, vln., & vcello.
- 150. 6 Pieces, vln. & organ.
- 151. Mass in G.
- 152. 30 Children's songs.
- 153. "Das Zauberwort," Singspiel, in 2 acts, for children.
- 154. 12th Organ sonata in D flat.
- 155. Mass, 3-part female choir, & organ.
- 156. 12 Characterstücke for organ.
- 157. 6 Sacred songs.
- 158.
- 159. Mass, 4-part choir and organ in F minor.
- 160. "Auf der Wanderung," 7 male choruses.
- 161. 13th Organ sonata, in E flat.
- 162. "Monologue," 12 organ pieces.
- 163. Five motets, 5-part choir.
- 164. "Die Stern von Bethlehem," Christmas cantata.
- 165. 14th Organ sonata, in C.
- 166. Suite, vln. & organ.
- 167. "Meditations," 12 organ pieces.

Op.
168. 15th Organ sonata, in D.
169. Mass, soli, choir, & orch.
170.
171. "Marianische Hymnen," voice & organ.
172. Mass, male choir & orch.
173. 4 Male choruses.
174.
175. 17th Organ sonata, in G sharp minor.

Without opus-numbers :—
    "Ave, Maria," soprano & organ.
    Romance for soprano & harp.
    "Carmina sacra," songs with organ.
    Arrangement of Bach's 30 variations for 2 pfs.

THE OLDER GENERATION

THEODOR KIRCHNER—CARL REINECKE—WOLDEMAR BARGIEL

THE two composers whose names stand first at the head of this chapter afford a curious parallel and a still more curious contrast to each other. Each has been so wholly possessed by admiration of a great master a little older and a great deal more richly endowed with genius than himself as to lose to a great extent his own artistic personality in that of his ideal. In early life THEODOR KIRCHNER took Schumann as the model of his life's work, and Reinecke in the same way took Mendelssohn.

The contrast between the outward circumstances of the great men has been strangely repeated in the lives of their respective followers; Reinecke seems to have inherited the prosperity and good fortune that were Mendelssohn's, while to Kirchner has fallen an undue share of trouble, though not of the same kind as that which darkened Schumann's days. It is only fair to add that Kirchner has inherited at the same time a double portion of Schumann's spirit.

Born December 10, 1823,* at Neukirchen in Saxony, Kirchner, the son of a schoolmaster in very humble circumstances, was brought up at Wittgensdorf, where, at a very early age, he began to learn the organ from his father. In 1831 he was taken to Dresden to be introduced, as a promising musical genius, to J. G. Schneider, an organist, the brother of the composer of "Das Weltgericht" —an oratorio that, whatever its worth, is perhaps more famous in the present day from the fact that Schumann, when a boy, got up a performance of it, than for any other reason. After learning what he could from the Bürgerschule at Chemnitz, Kirchner was taken to Leipzig, and presented to Weinlig and Mendelssohn, the latter of whom was delighted with the boy's powers of

* The date given in Grove and elsewhere, 1824, is wrong, as the certificate of birth, in the possession of Herr Constantin Sander, of Leipzig, shows the above to be the true date.

THEODOR KIRCHNER

extemporising on a given theme. He remained at Leipzig, studying with K. F. Becker, organist of the Nicolaikirche. Here the works of Schumann, who was then comparatively unknown, began to influence him, and in his own attempts at composition he naturally formed himself on the composer whom he admired. Both in Schumann's letters, and in his contributions to the *Neue Zeitschrift für Musik*, the favourable references to Kirchner's early works are numerous and most encouraging. Looking back upon Kirchner's career, Schumann's opinion of his powers seems a little exaggerated; but we know that he was the kindliest of critics and often mistook promise for actual attainment.

After a year at Dresden, where he went to complete his organ-studies under Schneider, Kirchner returned to Leipzig at the request of Mendelssohn, to enter the newly founded Conservatorium as its first pupil. In the autumn of 1843, after six months at the new school, he received his first appointment as organist at Winterthür, where he remained for nearly twenty years. He was succeeded, on his departure for Zürich, where he went to conduct the subscription concerts, by Hermann Goetz, the illustrious composer of the "Taming of the Shrew." Kirchner took part as organist at many musical festivals of considerable importance in Switzerland; his knowledge of "registration" is said to be one of his most remarkable qualities in this way, and it is one that is extremely rare among German organists. After a short residence at the ducal Court of Meiningen, he was appointed director of the newly-founded music-school in Würzburg, in February 1873; but two years of this kind of work were enough for him, and he went back to Leipzig in order to devote himself to composition and private lessons. Unfortunately these latter were so few that the composer's circumstances rapidly became serious: and at last, in desperation, he had to take to a means of livelihood which has often been resorted to by necessitous musicians—that of making pianoforte arrangements of popular works. It is only fair to say that he avoided the perpetration of this class of "pot-boiler" work as long as it was possible. Meanwhile his original compositions were long in making their way, and even now it cannot be said that they have received the attention they deserve. An appointment as teacher of ensemble-playing and score-reading at the Dresden Conservatorium, bestowed upon Kirchner in 1883, did not mend matters very much, for lessons were still very few; and in 1884 a subscription of some 36,000 marks was raised, by the energies of a committee of his friends, including Brahms, Stockhausen, Joachim, Bülow, and others. Since 1890 Kirchner has lived in Hamburg.

His works, the list of which now extends to op. 90, were at first very slowly produced; his op. 1 appeared in 1843, op. 2 not till 1850, and by 1870 only op. 10 had been reached. This points to a remarkable degree of self-criticism, and the same rare quality is to be perceived in the works themselves, which are always most carefully finished and maturely considered. Just as August Roeckel, when Capellmeister at Dresden, destroyed an opera of his own which had been accepted for performance, because he was overwhelmed by the greatness of Wagner's genius, so Kirchner dreaded publishing anything of his composition because he was only too fully conscious of his inferiority to Schumann. The disciple's music receives a strong colouring from that of the master, as is perhaps only natural; still, there are many features of distinct charm and even individuality. The great bulk of his work is in the form of songs and short pieces for pianoforte or violin; the list contains also a "serenade" for piano, violin, and violoncello, and a string quartet. It may be doubted whether the direct imitation of Schumann in the character of the titles chosen for many of these pieces has not actually stood in the way of their popularity, instead of assisting it, as it was no doubt meant to do.

We are sometimes inclined to think of Germany as a country where possibly all men, and certainly all musicians, find their proper level; where offices are always filled with the most competent candidates, and the right man is, as a matter of course, put into the right place. There may be fewer round pegs in square holes among German musicians than among those of our own country, but in general the impression is by no means correct. If it were, then should the name of CARL REINECKE, who has held for upwards of thirty years the most important post in the most important musical centre of Germany, stand high above all his countrymen. With his performance of his duties as conductor of the famous Gewandhaus concerts in Leipzig, English readers have little to do; it is hardly to be maintained, however, that he is a perfect conductor. To conduct an orchestra with complete success demands many of the characteristics which go to make a great general, and these characteristics could hardly be suggested to a German in connection with Reinecke's name without exciting mirth. He has the qualities of his defects, and a gentle nature gives to the best of his compositions the value which they undoubtedly possess. When the list of a composer's published works reaches the formidable number of over two hundred separate compositions, cast in every imaginable form, it seems strange that so very few of them should find wide or lasting acceptance in the world of music. It is pretty certain that Reinecke will be remembered in the near future, not by his operas "König Manfred" or "Der Gouverneur von Tours," his symphonies, his chamber compositions, or even by his piano concerto in F sharp minor—a work in which he has appeared with success in England, and one which is a good deal more happily inspired than the bulk of his compositions—but by certain works he has written for children, such as the pretty cantatas, "Schneewittchen" and "Aschenbrödel," "Dornröschen," "Schneeweisschen und Rosenroth," and the like, and the many children's songs by which his name is endeared to thousands of small Germans. His works in the larger forms are reproached, and no doubt fairly enough, with poverty of invention and cold classicality, although he is master of the ordinary resources of the instruments for which he writes, as well as of the more scientific parts of music, such as counterpoint, canonic devices, and so forth. As an arranger of other men's work he is especially successful: a delightful instance of this is the "improvisata" for two pianos on a hackneyed gavotte by Gluck, in the course of which he introduces with great ingenuity a musette of Bach against the theme. He is not merely an admirably sympathetic accompanist, but a most highly accomplished pianist of the older school—a school unaffected by the pyrotechnics of a generation that is now in its turn passing away. To have heard one of Mozart's concertos played by Reinecke is a memorable experience in the lives of such musicians as are sufficiently trained to appreciate the consummate delicacy and artistic skill which the performance exhibits.

The exact cause of his want of success as a composer may be hard to determine, for many men not more original than he have succeeded where he has not. It may be that his career has been too uniformly prosperous.

CARL REINECKE

"Wer nie sein Brod mit Thränen ass,
   *   *   *   *   *   *   *
Der kennt euch nicht, ihr himmlischen Mächte."

Many a career outwardly as prosperous as his has been saved from the unenlightened condition that Goethe speaks of, by difficulties of which the world never hears, by throes of production or tortures of self-criticism; but in this case the enormous list of compositions shows that their creation cannot have cost their author many pangs of travail.

Born in 1824 at Altona, the son of a musician, Carl Heinrich Carsten* Reinecke began to learn the pianoforte at five years old, and at eight to compose. At twelve his first appearance as a player took place at a concert of the "Apollo-Verein" in his native place; and about the same time he perpetrated an overture embodying the "Marseillaise," the performance of which had the honour of being stopped by the authorities. After many successful appearances in Denmark and elsewhere, he made his bow to the Leipzig audience at a Gewandhaus concert, playing Mendelssohn's "Serenade and Allegro giojoso" in the presence of the composer, and,

* The words of some of his songs are signed with his second and third names alone.

as far as is known, to his complete satisfaction. This took place just fifty years ago, in the winter of 1843. It was a curious coincidence that at the first chamber concert in Leipzig in which he took part he should have played Schumann's quintet, and thus at first identified himself in some measure with the two masters whose influence has been strongest upon him throughout his life. The years between this appearance and his appointment to the post which he still holds were occupied with successful concert-tours, in the intervals of which he lived first at Copenhagen, until the death of Christian VIII. in 1848, and the subsequent appropriation of Holstein, his native province, by Prussia. During a stay of three months in Paris in 1851 he gave pianoforte lessons to Liszt's two daughters—a high testimony to that great virtuoso's appreciation of his powers. After this he was successively appointed teacher of composition and piano in the Cologne music-school under Hiller (1851), music director at Barmen (1854), and director ("Universitäts-musikdirector") of the Singakademie at Breslau (1858). During his tenure of this last office he instituted the orchestral concerts which are still prosperous and famous throughout Germany.

CARL REINECKE

In 1860 he was invited to become conductor of the Gewandhaus concerts in succession to Julius Rietz, who went to Dresden in that year. At the same time he became teacher of composition and the pianoforte in the Conservatorium, another post which he still holds. In October 1885, his completion of twenty-five years' service as director was celebrated by a performance of his "König Manfred" at the Opera, and by a concert consisting exclusively of his compositions. At the opening of the new Gewandhaus in 1884 he received the degree of doctor *honoris causâ* from the University of Leipzig. He is the recipient of many orders and honours of various kinds, the list of which would take up almost as much space as that of his compositions. It may be surmised that he would gladly part with some of these distinctions, if by so doing he could attain for his music a larger share of wider and more permanent popularity than it now enjoys.

It is a truism that the romanticists of one generation become the classics of the next; that the discoveries over which pedants shook their heads at first are before long transformed into accepted canons of the schools. The change usually takes place almost imperceptibly, as those who were, in their youth, fervent admirers of what was new reach an age at which the pedagogic manner is too easily assumed. It is always the followers of the innovators, never the innovators themselves, who undergo this transition from living enthusiasms to dryasdust formulæ. Such a transition can sometimes be observed in progress, as in the case of WOLDEMAR BARGIEL, in the course of whose career the admiration of the great master who dominated German music during his early life has gradually changed into a more or less cold and academic habit of mind and work. Outward causes have contributed largely to this, for his career as a teacher began immediately on the close of his pupilage, and for this reason, too, it is hardly to be wondered at if his own compositions have failed to make a very deep or permanent mark upon the art of his time.

With Schumann, the chief object of his musical adoration, he had more than an artistic connexion, since he is half-brother of Madame Schumann, whose mother, after being separated from Friedrich Wieck, married a musician named Bargiel. The composer was born in Berlin,

WOLDEMAR BARGIEL

October 3, 1828, and, like so many of his colleagues, received the rudiments of musical instruction on the piano, organ, and violin from his father, who was the founder of an institute on the Logier method in Berlin. On the death of his father his musical education must have stopped, the widow being unable to afford her son regular lessons, had it not been for the kindness of Herr Grell, the well-known director of the "Singakademie," through whose influence the boy was admitted into the probationary choir, and ultimately, as alto soloist, into the Domchor. He made good use of his time, and of the opportunities for more advanced instruction which came to him through Wilhelm Dehn; in 1846, having applied for it on Schumann's advice, he obtained the equivalent of a scholarship at the Leipzig Conservatorium, where for four years he studied with such excellent masters as Richter, Hauptmann, Rietz, Gade, and Moscheles, and where he wrote an octet for strings, performed with success at one of the concerts of the institution. He was enabled to remain at the Conservatorium longer than the regular time by a grant from the King of Prussia, and in 1850 he returned to Berlin as a pianoforte teacher, composing only in his spare time. Throughout his life, indeed, composition has been only the resource of his leisure, not the main employment of his time. With the change of residence seems to have come a change in artistic ideals, for Mendelssohn was no longer what he had been, prime favourite among composers; Schumann's influence, both personal and artistic, was upon the young man, and the promise given in his early works was hailed by the older musician with his usual warmth of expression.

In 1858 Bargiel received an invitation from Hiller to the post of pianoforte teacher at the Cologne Conservatorium, where he remained until 1865, when he was appointed director of the "Maatschappij tot Bevordering der Toonkunst" at Rotterdam; here he conducted the excellent concerts given by this energetic and useful society for some nine years, until he returned once more to Berlin as teacher of composition in the Royal Academy of Arts, a post which he held together with that of teacher of score- and ensemble-playing in the Hochschule. In 1875 he was made a member of the Academy; in 1878 he received the title of Royal Professor; in 1882 he became president of what is known as a Meisterschule, intended for advanced pupils only, and in 1888 president of the composition department of the Hochschule. Since 1875 he has conducted the Bach Society of Berlin.

The largest section of his works is that for pianoforte solo or duet, that instrument being alone concerned in 26 out of his 47 published compositions. He is at his best in these, for he excels in the invention of ingenious passages, and in the dexterous arrangement of ideas not often marked by individuality or exceptional beauty. The suite in G minor, op. 31, with its five well contrasted movements, is perhaps the most popular of these works, and it certainly deserves to be so. Its "Marcia fantastica" contains a curious instance of the amalgamation, or rather alternation, of two different and wholly contrasting movements in one, the device which adorns the middle movement of Brahms' violin sonata in A. Some of the author's most ambitious works, such as the symphony in C major, op. 30, suffer from a certain triviality in the thematic material, and a want of originality in its treatment. The working out of his subjects seems often to be done in an almost perfunctory way, as if from a sense of duty to the composer's pupils, rather than in obedience to any impulse of genius. The first of his three trios, op. 6, in F, is among the best of his works; dedicated to Schumann, it opens with a quotation from that master's quintet, treated canonically, and its subject-matter throughout is very beautiful. The grace of many of his slighter pieces, such as a particularly lovely "Albumblatt" in G major, and others, make it most unjust to describe Bargiel as academical, and nothing more. Of the three orchestral overtures, that to "Medea" is better than the "Overture to a Tragedy" (also called "Romeo and Juliet"), or that to "Prometheus." Four psalms for different choral combinations, with and without orchestra, represent his contribution to church music; and a group of six most graceful trios for female voices, opp. 35 and 39, have attained a well-deserved popularity. An essay of some interest on "Novelty in Music," which appeared in Lewinsky's "Vor den Coulissen," represents the composer's contribution to musical literature. If he cannot be classed with the greatest of the living masters, or look forward with certainty to a place among the immortals of music, it must be remembered in his favour that he has never fallen below a high artistic ideal, or courted popularity by work consciously of an inferior order. His influence has been wholly for good, and his success as a teacher undeniable.

TWO GREAT VIRTUOSI

JOSEPH JOACHIM—CLARA SCHUMANN

The present series of monographs does not pretend to deal with any class of musicians except composers; but it so happens that two of the most illustrious instrumental performers that Germany has ever produced are also two composers of high merit, one of them a creative genius of quite exceptional power. It is only just, then, to notice, however shortly, the career both of Joachim and Mme. Schumann as composers, leaving on one side the brilliant record of each in the sphere where each has made the greatest mark on the history of the art.

It is a rule of almost universal application that performers of rare dexterity are bound to make certain sacrifices to that dexterity, and at least to make it the chief element in their artistic career. By dexterity I do not mean merely superficial agility of finger or of voice, but the whole technical side of the performer's art. This side of music acquires such an attraction for them that they are apt to neglect not only the other branches of music itself, but all the rest of the intellectual life. The better members of the virtuoso class are frequently to be found among the composers, but in nearly all cases their compositions, if not actually and intentionally show-pieces for their own use, are almost sure to be affected in some way or other by that particular quality in which they excel as performers. Liszt is an instance of a brilliant performer who cultivated other developments of music, besides those which concerned the pianoforte, and his contributions to the new effects of orchestration are of permanent value, though his original creations are as a rule far less excellent than his manifold transcriptions and arrangements of various kinds. In these, or rather in many of them, even where the pianoforte is not employed at all, the figures seem often to have been suggested by pianoforte passages, and his extraordinary lack of the sense of beauty in melody may be in some sort accounted for by the

JOSEPH JOACHIM

damaging effect upon the musical ear of certain branches of piano practice. JOSEPH JOACHIM is the very reverse of all this. If the greater number of his exceedingly small list of compositions are for the violin, and if they naturally include works of "transcendental" difficulty (as it is the fashion to call them), there are also many whose musical value is entirely independent of the instrument on which the master has so long ago gained his complete supremacy.

He does not, like Schumann, deliberately shun "effect," but no writer has ever shown a more complete disregard of what will please the public. In this way, as in so many others, Joachim stands alone amongst virtuosi, for in each and all of his works art is the first thing considered. On a certain memorable occasion, when a large number of his admirers in England presented him with a Stradivarius violin of historic celebrity, after a "Monday Pop," he made a little speech, at the end of which he stated his conviction that the musician's ideal should be "to uphold the dignity of art." This high object has in the fullest sense been realised by him, whether in his illustrious career as a player, or in his less prominent capacity as a composer.

Born at Kittsee, near Pressburg, June 28, 1831, the youngest of a family of seven, he played the violin at five years old, and was very early placed under Szervacsinsky, the leader of the opera band at Pesth, for instruction. From 1841 onwards he was a pupil of Böhm in Vienna, receiving from him the traditions of the greatest school of violin-playing, that had been handed down in an unbroken line from Corelli. At twelve years old he visited North Germany for the first time, appearing at Leipzig at a concert given by Mme. Viardot on May 14, 1843; he played a rondo by De Beriot, Mendelssohn himself doing him the honour of playing the accompaniment. The Leipzig musical atmosphere suited the boy's earnest nature, and here under David he laid the foundations of his wonderful power of interpreting the classical masterpieces, while he studied composition under Hauptmann, and learnt much from his intimacy with Mendelssohn. When he came to London, in 1844, he was in some senses a finished artist. It is odd to think of his making his first bow to an English audience under the auspices of the "poet Bunn," at whose benefit concert he appeared on March 28. A more satisfactory

JOSEPH JOACHIM

engagement at the Philharmonic followed in two months' time, and he played there Beethoven's immortal concerto. It may be almost said that ever since then England has been a second home to him all through his artistic career; his visits did not become annual, however, until the establishment of the Popular Concerts. In 1849, through the recommendation of his countryman, Franz Liszt, he received the appointment of leader of the Grand Duke's band at Weimar, but the "advanced" or revolutionary theories which were then beginning to make themselves felt in the music of the place were by no means congenial to him, and in 1854 he accepted the post of solo-violinist to the King of Hanover. Here he remained until 1866, and here he married the famous contralto singer, Amalie Weiss, in 1863. In 1868 he was made head of the "Hochschule für ausübende Tonkunst" at Berlin, a post in which he has exercised a splendid influence on the younger generation ever since.

It may well be imagined that there would not be much time for composition in a life taken up with perpetual appearances in public and constant teaching, to say nothing of the management of a great school of music. There would have been no cause to grumble if his work as a composer had been confined to a few trifling violin solos, attractive because played by their author in unsurpassable style, but disappointing in other hands. With that sort of thing we are only too familiar. But with Joachim the case is different; his compositions are none of them trifles, and those which are for the violin he most rarely plays, at least in England. The list is somewhat remarkable, for the extremely small number of small things in it, and for the large proportion of important works:—

Op.
1. Andantino and allegro scherzoso, vln. & orch.
2. Three pieces (Romance, " Fantasiestück," " Frühlingsfantasie "), vln. & pf.
3. Concerto in G minor for vln. & orch.
4. Overture to " Hamlet," orch.
5. Three pieces ("Lindenrauschen," "Abendglocken," Ballade), vln. & pf.
6. Overture to Schiller's " Demetrius," unpublished.
7. Overture to " Henry IV.," unpublished at present.
8. Overture to a play by Gozzi, unpublished.
9. Hebrew melodies for viola and pf.
10. Variations on an original theme, viola and pf.
11. Hungarian concerto in D minor, vln. & orch.
12. Notturno in A, vln. & small orch.
13. Overture in memory of Kleist.
14. Scena, "Marfa" from Schiller's *Demetrius*, contralto & orch.

JOSEPH JOACHIM

Two marches, in C and D respectively.
Romance for violin & pianoforte.
Variations in E minor, vln. & orch.
Concerto in G major (written soon after the "Hungarian Concerto," but only lately published).
Song, " Ich hab im Traum geweinet."
Song, " Rain, Rain, and Sun," written for an album of settings of Tennyson.
Cadenzas for Beethoven's concerto.
The cadenza in Brahms' violin concerto, intended for Joachim, is said to have been written by the player.

These works, whatever their calibre, have certain strongly marked characteristics in common. At first hearing they are often a little obscure, and at times even forbidding and on the surface harsh. The long-drawn sweetness of the romance from op. 2, or of the slow movement of the Hungarian concerto, is a quality not very often met with elsewhere, and the sombre mien of the Kleist overture seems to have more attractions for the composer. On a closer acquaintance the real grandeur of his ideas, and the passionate ardour which seems to be the result of his Hungarian parentage, make themselves felt, and the complete command of musical structure which all the works reveal is very remarkable in a man who has after all written so little. The masterpiece among the compositions is undoubtedly the Hungarian concerto, which in the perfect proportion between its national themes and the original matter, in its exquisite treatment of the solo instrument as well as of the orchestra, and in its rare and captivating beauty, stands alone among works of the kind. It contains, in the cadenza of the first movement, an effect which never loses its electrifying impression, however often it is heard. In the course of its embroideries on the themes of the movement, the solo instrument seems to call forth one after another of the accompanying instruments, each of which enters, at first in unison with the violin, so that each is playing for a moment or two before its presence is detected; the impression produced, upon some listeners at all events, is that of a magician who evokes one spirit after another to do his bidding. Next to this superb work I am inclined to place the concerto in G major, in which the first movement has, in its breadth and smoothness of melodic construction, some characteristics of the best English music about it. The variations in E minor have this disadvantage—that in any one's hands but the composer's they cannot but sound scratchy, and even crabbed in construction.

JOSEPH JOACHIM

In only three of the works mentioned above is the human voice employed; in the scena set to a passage in Schiller's unfinished play a very remarkable degree of dramatic force is displayed in the treatment of the voice, and it is clear that, if he had chosen or had had time and opportunity, Joachim might have written a fine opera. By the setting of Merlin's song there hangs a tale which illustrates both the composer's true instinct in the setting of words even in a language not his own, and a great poet's intuitive recognition of musical merit. When the album spoken of above was first published, an eminent English musician, who was a friend of Tennyson's, went through the songs for the poet's benefit; it is well known that Tennyson was as little of a practical musician as a man can be, and that in particular he had a rooted objection to musical settings of his own songs, giving as the reason for this that the music always went up when he wanted it to go down, and down when he wanted it to go up. From the whole book of songs he selected those which seemed to fall in with his ideas of what the melody should be, and the performer noticed with much interest that the poet, though ignorant of the names of the composers as the songs were gone through, pronounced favourably upon precisely those songs which a trained musician would have chosen if he had the list of composers before him. Joachim's song was one of those most warmly praised. It is strange that so great a master of concerted music, perhaps the greatest quartet-leader the world has ever seen, should have contributed nothing to music of this class; nor is it now likely that the omission will be repaired, since the composer has stated his intention of writing no more, as his teaching and playing take up too much time.

The outward appearance of Joachim is so familiar to English amateurs that no reference need be made to it. His rapt look as he stands absorbed in some suite by Bach, or some other work that he loves, is as well known to us as to his countrymen, and is as familiar as the famous lock of hair, now slightly grey, that falls over his eyes. Concerning this, the story, afterwards inserted in *Punch*, with, of course, a face of Mr. Du Maurier's invention attached to it, is absolutely true—that a Kensington hairdresser, when performing on the great violinist, strongly recommended the removal of this lock, saying: "It makes you look just like one o' them fiddling fellows."

JOSEPH JOACHIM

The revelation of personal character in musical performances is a science which has yet to be studied; but only those who know Joachim and his playing most intimately can tell how exactly the one is the counterpart of the other. A nobler character it would scarcely be possible to imagine; generous, full of sympathy, tender with the great tenderness of a great nature, yet firm as a rock where any principle, artistic or otherwise, is concerned. To say that the admiration which has been his throughout his life has left him entirely unspoilt is very meagre praise, since artists of the highest calibre not seldom possess the power of going through the world unscathed by adulation, and, indeed, partially unconscious of it. A great sorrow, which a few years since darkened his life, broke up a home which had been the centre of all that was best in the musical life of Germany, and for a time seemed to have affected his playing, in however slight a degree; as time has gone on, even this has been turned to artistic good, and recently his playing has a pathos more profound, a sympathy more wide, and if I may venture to say so, a style more mature, than ever before.

It is quite certain that if some accident had

deprived Joachim of the use of his hands as a violinist, he would have attained a very high position among composers; that CLARA SCHUMANN would have done so, in a similar case, can perhaps be less positively asserted, although the quality of her music is undoubtedly so high as to make it impossible to omit her name from a list of the best composers of Germany. The tiny list of her compositions contains things of such deep feeling, such real power, and such high attainment, that in strict justice no account of German music in the present day could be complete without a reference to them. Still, supposing her to have been isolated from the pianoforte, one does not feel that composition would have been a permanent necessity of her existence; and the wifely devotion which was so beautiful a trait in her character is carried into the music she wrote to such an extent that the common reproach—that it is merely a reflection of her husband's work—is widely accepted, although as a matter of fact it is by no means true. To superficial observers there may seem to be no elements of real individuality, apart from the great composer with whom she was allied, just as the same class of critics are in the habit of denying to

Sterndale Bennett originality apart from Mendelssohn. Both assertions are equally false.

This is not the place to recapitulate the events of Mme. Schumann's career as a pianist, or to dwell upon the exquisite qualities in her playing which have made her by far the greatest artist in her own direction among pianists of all periods. In this connexion it may be said of her, as of Joachim, that she has not only touched nothing that she did not adorn, but has touched nothing that was not worthy of her position as a supreme artist. Of how many public performers can the same be said? Her perfect technique, her marvellous power of tone-gradation, and the romantic expressiveness of her touch, were simply used as means to an end, and that end was, not to glorify herself, but to explain to her hearers the full meaning of the music she "interpreted" (the well-worn word was true of her as it has been true of very few musicians of any kind). Few missions have been so completely fulfilled as that which she set herself, when still quite young, of bringing home to musicians the works of her illustrious husband. She has truly "seen of the travail of her soul," and the universal recognition of Schumann's genius which long ago succeeded to the shameful and persistent ignoring of his powers, is due in no small measure to her perseverance in the early days. The necessity for forcing her audiences, as it were, to see, in spite of the critics, what there was in her husband's music, may well have stimulated the gift of interpretation, in the same way that the wonderful and unapproachable depth and intensity of her style must have been increased, though not altogether caused, by the long succession of troubles of different kinds which have been her companions almost throughout her life. Bitter anxiety and distressing illness—these she has known intimately, although, of course, there have been many bright days in her life, and such an artistic career as hers must be a source of very real pleasure, whether at the time or in retrospect.

Born September 13, 1819, Clara Wieck made her first appearance in public soon after her ninth birthday; her regular appearances can scarcely be said to have begun until 1832, from which time onwards she was a constant performer at the Gewandhaus concerts of her native town, Leipzig. The romantic story of her marriage with Robert Schumann in 1840, after a terrible amount of difficulties placed in the way by her father, is one of the best-known incidents of musical history. It was just before her husband's tragic death in 1856 that she made her first appearance in London, where the most prominent musical critics vied with each other in indecent abuse of the compositions which she was most anxious to make popular. It cannot have been much consolation to her to read the somewhat halfhearted praises of her own performances, side by side with scurrilous witticisms on Schumann's music, or to know that the person who held the highest position on the musical press happened to be the husband of a lady who was supposed to be a rival of Mme. Schumann's. Happily the episode (one of the least agreeable in the musical history of our country) was afterwards amply atoned for in the brilliant successes of her appearances in subsequent years. From 1865 to 1882 her visits were annual, excepting the years 1866, 1878, 1879, and 1880. She came again every year from 1885 to 1888 inclusive, and each year her reception was more and more cordial. From 1878 till 1892 she was principal teacher of the pianoforte at the Hoch Conservatorium in Frankfort, resigning her post at last on account of bad health. It is difficult to imagine any form of disease more distressing to a musician than an affection of the auditory nerve which causes the sensation of continually hearing musical sounds entirely unconnected with any music that may be actually going on. It is a curious coincidence that for some time in his later life Schumann heard a persistent A in the same way, which, of course, entirely prevented his enjoying music at all; it is most welcome news that Mme. Schumann has latterly lost the terrible *obsession* to which she was at one time subject, and which she has described as a continual series of "sequences."

In a life so full of other interests and occupations—for in her later years Mme. Schumann has thrown herself heart and soul into the highest branches of pianoforte-teaching, with the greatest possible success—it may readily be imagined that not much time was left for composition; still, the main reason for the excessive smallness of the list of her works is probably to be found in a certain artistic fastidiousness which prevented her giving to the world anything that was not representative of her work at its very best. That self-criticism which so very few, even of the best composers, possess is hers in a very high degree, and it has, no doubt, tended to keep down the number of her published compositions. Here is the list, taken in the main from Grove's Dictionary:

Op.
1. 4 Polonaises, for pf.
2. Caprices en forme de valses, for pf.
3. Romance variée, for pf.
4. "Valses Romantiques," for pf.
5.⎱
6.⎰ "Soirées musicales," 10 characteristic pieces, for pf.
7. Concerto for pf. and orch. in A minor.
8. Concert variations on a theme from Bellini's "Pirata," for pf.
9. "Souvenir de Vienne," for pf.
10. Scherzo in D minor, for pf.
11. 3 Romances for pf.
12. 5 Songs, included in Schumann's op. 37, from Rückert's "Liebesfrühling."
13. 6 Songs.
14. Scherzo for pf., No. 2.
15. 4 Fugitive pieces, for pf.
16. 3 Preludes and fugues for pf.
17. Trio, pf. & strings in G minor.
18.⎱ These numbers seem to have been passed over
19.⎰ from inadvertence.
20. Variations on a theme by Robert Schumann (No. 4 of his "Bunte Blätter," op. 99), for pf.
21. 3 Romances for pf.
22. 3 Romances for pf. and violin.
23. 6 Songs from Rollet's "Jucunde."

Andante and allegro, pf.
Cadenzas to Beethoven's concertos in C minor and G, & to Mozart's in D minor.

The theme of her op. 3 was used by her husband as that of his eleven impromptus, op. 5; the so-called "motto" of his "Davidsbündlertänze," and two themes in the sonata in F minor, op. 14, are also by the wife, and occur—the motto in her mazurka, op. 6, No. 5, and the sonata themes in the fourth piece of op. 5, called "Le Ballet des Revenants."

These and other subjects by her have a directness and simplicity, combined with a dignity of demeanour, that are characteristic of Mme. Schumann's compositions, as indeed they are of her playing. The actual workmanship of her trio, and the scholarly construction of her fugues, reveal the earnest student, and her cadenzas, while brilliant and effective, are always in keeping with the works they adorn. Her work, I venture to think, reaches its highest point in the songs written for joint production by herself (as her op. 12) and her husband (as his op. 37). The three lyrics, "Er ist gekommen in Sturm und Regen," "Liebst du um Schönheit?" and "Warum willst du And're fragen?" may not reach the tragic depth of expression of her husband's "Ich grolle nicht," or touch the heights of spiritualised passion with his

"Widmung"; but for a parallel to their revelation of the purest and most ardent love of a woman's soul we must look away from music altogether to the "Sonnets from the Portuguese" of Mrs. Browning. In beauty of theme and treatment, and in those qualities which are rightly extolled as of the essence of a perfect lyric, these songs are surpassed by few of the greatest creations of the greatest songwriters, Schubert, Schumann, Franz, or Brahms. The first of these three is sometimes heard, and the delicious little link between it and the next, "O ihr Herren" (by Robert Schumann) more seldom; "Liebst du um Schönheit?" is unaccountably neglected by singers, for it is pre-eminently effective in the hands of an intelligent artist. The third of Mme. Schumann's contributions, the concluding song of the album, has a remarkable foreshadowing of a passage in "Er der herrlichste von Allen" at the words "Sondern sieh' die Augen an."

As the perfect lyric is the flower and crown of the poet's attainment, the song that reaches perfection in music is the infallible mark of high genius, perhaps even more sure than the larger forms, in which so much may be accomplished by well-trained mediocrity. If this be true, then should Mme. Schumann's place among German composers be in the highest rank, even had she written nothing but these exquisite songs.

THE LITTLE MASTERS

HEINRICH VON HERZOGENBERG— HEINRICH HOFMANN——ANTON BRUCKNER——FELIX DRAESEKE

IT may be permitted to borrow from a sister art a convenient term that has long been recognised as indicating a class of men, belonging to various schools, whose productions are not striking enough to win them a great name in history, although they contain such excellences as make it impossible to ignore them or to regard them as in a state of pupilage to the school of which they are members. A group of such composers demands notice in any complete account of contemporary art, and it is particularly necessary in dealing with German composers of the present day, since, with the one great exception, the living musicians stand so nearly on a level that to single out a few names for detailed notice would be invidious and unfair. The lovers of the purely classical school, whether in its earlier or later developments, will agree to assign the first place in such a group to HEINRICH VON HERZOGENBERG, who is not only looked upon by German purists as one of the few defenders of the orthodox faith, but is also held up as one of the still fewer converts from a Wagnerism more or less pronounced.

Heinrich von Herzogenberg was born at Graz, June 10, 1843, and after some elementary musical instruction entered the Vienna Conservatorium in 1862, remaining there for three years under the late Otto Dessoff, the well-known conductor of the Frankfort Opera, and a musician of the widest sympathies. At the close of the school curriculum, Herzogenberg returned to Graz, in order to devote himself almost entirely to composition. His comparatively late adoption of a serious musical career may have had something to do with the freedom and certainty of intention which distinguish even his first published compositions. As I have said, in early life he was an ardent Wagnerian, and two of the most ambitious productions of this part of his career are unmistakably influenced by the newer methods. In particular this is the case with the "Odysseus" symphony, op. 16, and "Columbus," a dramatic cantata for solos, choir, and orchestra, op. 11. This latter is a most remarkable work, if we consider that it was a first experiment in orchestral composition. It is full of picturesque passages, and sections, such as the sailors' choruses, that have a frank, manly character, though it can hardly be maintained that the cantata has the unity which is indispensable in works that are to live. At Graz he married Elizabeth Stockhausen, an accomplished pianist and a composer of some attainment. In 1872, feeling a not unnatural dearth of musical opportunities in Styria, the couple transferred themselves to Leipzig. The intimacy which he ormed with Volkland, Spitta, and von Holstein resulted in the formation of a Bach Society which has since become famous, and to the same cause may, no doubt, be assigned the pronounced change in the composer's musical opinions; the close study of Bach's works, and in particular of the church cantatas, a set of which Herzogenberg edited in piano score, effected what one party in Germany regarded as his cure from the dangerous tenets into which he had been led. On Volkland's removal to Basle, Herzogenberg suceeded him as conductor of the society, and from this time a severe and more dignified tone became apparent in his own work. An arrangement for chorus of a number of old German Volkslieder, made about this time, show that the influence of Wagner had almost, if not entirely, been overcome. In 1885 he was summoned to Berlin to help Kiel in the Hochschule, and on Kiel's death in the same year the younger man was given the post and title of professor of composition. Unfortunately he was obliged to resign the office after about a year's work, in consequence of ill-health; after trying various German baths he went to Nice, where he spent the greater part of two years. Having recovered his health, he returned to Berlin, and was appointed director of the " Academische Meisterschule " for composition. In 1890 he received the much coveted distinction of election to the Academy, subsequently becoming a member of the senate of that body. Once more he was compelled to give up his professorial work, owing to his wife's health. Since her death in Italy, he has lived in that country; but has not yielded to the temptation to over-production, which few composers set free from routine work would have resisted.

It has been maintained by an eminent German critic that Herzogenberg has not yet reached the highest point of his development; this may very well be the case, although it is a little unsafe to commit oneself to such an opinion. He certainly has not as yet manifested any strong individuality in his music, for his recent works are as plainly influenced by Brahms as those of his green youth were by Wagner. Still, if a man has not reached to the expression of his own personality by the time he is fifty years old, there seems but slight chance of his arriving at any very high point. At the same time, the skilful workmanship and the completely artistic style which mark his compositions, entitle them to a high place in the estimation of musicians; and if he has not evinced any remarkable degree of originality, he is at all events no plagiarist. In the opinion of German connoisseurs, Herzogenberg's best works are those for choir, notably his setting of Psalm cxvi. for four-part chorus *a capella*, with its three contrasting yet homogeneous sections, and Psalm xciv. in which a quartet of soloists and the organ are added to the double choir and orchestra. Two odes, "Der Stern des Lieds" op. 55, and "Die Weihe der Nacht," op. 56, have much nobility of character, and among the numerous songs are many that reach a high standard of beauty and refined expression. A finely conceived setting of the Requiem Mass, op. 72, is among the best of the composer's recent works; it was suggested by the death of Frau von Herzogenberg. Of the smaller vocal works, the graceful "Deutsches Liederspiel," op. 14, and a set of four Notturnos, op. 22, are deservedly popular, and perhaps not the less that they shew traces of the influence of Brahms' "Liebeslieder." In England Herzogenberg's name is hardly known, except as the composer of three violin sonatas, the first of which, an effective and scholarly work, has been occasionally played in public by Joachim, who is a great friend of the composer. A quintet for pianoforte and wind-instruments has been brought forward by the Wind Instrument Chamber Music Society, and a string quartet at the Popular Concerts, but of the rest of his concerted music English amateurs know as little as they do of his two symphonies, opp. 50 and 70.

The remark which has often been made with regard to Sterndale Bennett's music, that it is

HEINRICH HOFMANN

essentially that of a gentleman, is particularly true of Herzogenberg's work: an almost excessive degree of refinement, of fastidious self-criticism, stand revealed in his compositions—qualities which, admirable as they are, must to some extent hinder them from becoming widely popular. It is, perhaps, inevitable that they should lack breadth and boldness, but "finish" is so rare a quality in these days, at least with all but the very greatest masters, that for its sake much may be excused.

If Herzogenberg's music is essentially the music of a gentleman, that of HEINRICH HOFMANN is in like manner indicative of the author's origin. It is evidently written with a view to popularity, and at times he seems to be seeking for the position of purveyor of the people's music, that position which has hardly been filled in Germany since the death of Nessler. There is generally a *bourgeois* flavour about it, and, occasionally, plebeian seems the only word to apply. It is, of course, a mere coincidence that the composer's social status was not very high in early life, and it is entirely to his credit that he has succeeded in making for himself an honourable place among the musicians of Germany. His father was a poor artisan who wandered from Bamberg to Berlin; in the latter city the composer was born, January 13, 1842. A childhood spent in sickness and poverty was relieved by one divine gift—that of a beautiful soprano voice. This attracting the attention of Herr Bader, a member of the Hofoper company, and a "heroic tenor" by profession, the boy was admitted into the choir of the cathedral in 1851, and after two years was entrusted with the solo work there. The church pay, small as it was, suggested to the boy's father that he might enter the Church in a higher capacity, and this in spite of very decided disinclination for the priesthood on the son's part. As usual the musical bent was too strong, and young Hofmann was receiving a considerable amount of training and experience, both from his position in the choir, which made him acquainted with the works of Palestrina, Bach, Handel, and others, and, in another branch of art, from an engagement in the opera chorus, where he was employed from 1853 to 1856. A piano was bought for twelve thalers, and a kind-hearted pupil of the Conservatorium was induced to give him gratuitous lessons. On the breaking of his voice he ceased, as a matter of course, to earn money, and it is difficult to see what would have become of his musical education if it had not been for Theodor Kullak, the eminent pianoforte-teacher, who undertook the lad's tuition for an almost nominal sum. A certain amount of lessons to be given to less advanced performers came in his way through his intercourse with the well-known teacher, and as time went on other branches of music were mastered by the help of some of the best professors in Berlin—Grell, who imbued him with a taste for the noblest school of Italian church music, Dehn, who taught him counterpoint, and Wüerst, who instructed him in score-reading. A considerable number of more or less experimental compositions, written now, were committed to the flames in later years; the first success, and that not a very brilliant one, was with a one-act opera, "Cartouche," op. 7. A Hungarian Suite for orchestra, op. 16—almost a first attempt at purely orchestral writing—drew the attention of the public at large to the young composer, and as an illustration of what popularity means in Germany it may be mentioned that it was given upwards of 100 times in the year 1873 alone, and that in good concerts. His next compositions were, of course, successful. Among them are a "Champagnerlied" for male choir and orchestra; a trio in A for a piano and strings, op. 18; "Nornengesang" for female choir and orchestra, op. 21, and a symphony, "Frithjof," op. 22. This last was played upwards of seventy times in 1874, after its production under Bilse's direction. It is an effective piece, more or less closely conforming to the type of "programme music," and dealing mainly with the loves of Frithjof and Ingeborg; it relies for its local colour on a scherzo called "Elves of light and rock-giants." A string sextet, many songs and piano pieces, an "overture to a comedy," and other things, separate this, in the composer's list, from a cantata for soli, choir and orchestra, "Die schöne Melusine," a work which soon went the rounds of choral societies in Germany, succeeding in general popularity the "Erl King's Daughter" of Gade. A four-act opera, "Armin," after a poem of Felix Dahn, was produced in Dresden in 1877 and spread to most of the German opera-houses. The success of these works was such as to enable him to give up teaching altogether, an occupation in which he had been much engaged and with considerable success. His second grand opera, "Aennchen von Tharau," in three acts, produced in 1878 at Hamburg, was revived in the spring of last year at Schwerin and received with remarkable favour. "Aschenbrödel" (Cinderella), for soli, choir and orchestra, has also been successfully given in Europe and America, and a number of smaller works, belonging to the same period, illustrate the ceaseless activity which is one of Hofmann's chief characteristics, and one which, it may be, has hindered his advance to higher artistic levels than he has attained. The cold reception of "Wilhelm von Oranien," an opera in three acts, at Hamburg on Feb. 5, 1882, must have been a strange experience for one whom success has followed almost slavishly; an unsatisfactory performance is said to have been the immediate cause, and the unfavourable verdict was reversed at Dantzig not long afterwards. Two sets of songs from Wolff's poem "Singuf," opp. 59 and 60; a piano quartet, op. 50; and some graceful serenades, preceded the production of his next opera, "Donna Diana," in three acts, brought out at Berlin in November 1886. "Im Schlosshof," an orchestral suite, op. 78, is a sufficiently picturesque piece of work, and is considered one of the composer's best achievements. "Lenz and Liebe," a cycle in "Liebeslieder" form, op. 84; "Irrlichter und Kobolde," an orchestral scherzo, op. 94; "Editha," a cantata, op. 100, and "Johanna von Orleans," another choral work, with solo parts, op. 105, are among Hofmann's most recent works, the latest of which is yet another cantata on the subject of Prometheus, op. 110.

An amazing facility in manufacturing music, complete mastery in expressing what he desires to express, an absence of such originality as might offend the public, and an entire lack of distinction, are the chief characteristics of Hofmann's music, and perhaps among the chief causes of its success with the German people. The composer has been freely "decorated": he was made a member of the Berlin Academy in 1882, and has been given the title of Professor by the Grand Duke of Mecklenburg-Schwerin. In his prosperous career it is not probable that he has been visited by qualms as to his ultimate position in the history of music, and he is no doubt to be envied for many reasons.

To include among the "little masters" a man who has written eight symphonies, one of which suffices for an entire concert, is, perhaps, to stretch the term to its utmost limits; but, judging from the quality and value of his work, rather than by its pretensions, ANTON BRUCKNER finds here his legitimate place. The composer is one who must command the respect of all true lovers of art, for he has worked for art's sake alone with a singleness of purpose and a real unworldliness that are entirely estimable. He has waited long for his reward, but in later years he has obtained a great measure of recognition, and if that recognition is mainly found in one section of the German musical world, it is the section which, no doubt, Bruckner is most anxious to please. He is the symphonist of the extreme Wagnerians, who consider him to possess that small portion of Beethoven's spirit which failed to descend upon the Bayreuth master. So late has his day been in coming that it is difficult to realise that he has recently entered upon his 70th year.

Born at Ansfelden in Upper Austria, September 4, 1824, Bruckner began to study music under his father, a village schoolmaster, when he was nine years of age. About three years later the death of the father left the family in extreme poverty, and the prelate of St. Florian, a Jesuit college at Kalksburg, gave the boy a free berth on that foundation, as a chorister. His musical education was well looked after, for not only did he learn the violin from a certain Gruber, a pupil of Schuppanzigh, known to readers of the Beethoven literature, but he was taught harmony and counterpoint, and had lessons from Dürrnberger at Linz. In 1841 he received his first appointment, as a school-teacher at Windhag, with the incredible salary of two florins a month—*i.e.*, considerably less than a shilling a week. He managed to scrape along somehow by playing dance-music at weddings, etc., for 25 kreuzer (about 6*d.*) a night. In 1845 he returned to Kalksburg as deputy organist and teacher, and in 1851 became principal organist, with an annual salary of £8, and an additional salary as teacher of £3 12*s.* His post gave him plenty of opportunities for the composition of sacred music, and many masses, psalms, etc., date from this time. He also visited Vienna, and ultimately became pupil of the famous Sechter for counterpoint and composition. He attracted the notice of the best musical authorities by his astonishing powers of improvisation, and his extemporaneous performance of a regularly-constructed fugue on the organ procured him the place of cathedral organist at Linz in 1855. He continued his studies in Vienna, and in 1861 the authorities of the Conservatorium gave him a certificate of proficiency. For two years after this, so wanting was he in the false pride which academical success too often generates, he studied orchestration with Otto Kitzler, a man ten years his junior, and in 1864 his first symphony was played at Linz. In 1867 he was appointed professor of the organ, harmony and counterpoint at the Vienna Conservatorium, and in the following year he succeeded his old master, Sechter, as Court organist. (Sechter, it will be remembered, was the master of J. L. Hatton, and of many other distinguished musicians.) Bruckner's fame as an organist had spread so far that in 1869 he visited Paris, after a successful competition at Nancy, and gave recitals there, and was invited in 1871 to give recitals on the new organ in the Albert Hall in connection with the International Exhibition of that year. The fame of his extempore playing was used, most injudiciously, as a "puff preliminary," and, as a natural result, some critics were disappointed. The *Monthly Musical Record* of September 1871, remarks: "Herr

Bruckner is a very respectable player; but really great improvisations are productions peculiar to genius, and of that we perceived no proof." At the same time due allowance has to be made for the difficulty of managing a strange organ effectively, especially when the curious acoustic properties of the hall at Kensington are considered. During the same visit to England, while he was playing at the Crystal Palace, he was so carried away by the course of his ideas in improvisation that the exhausted blowers could not maintain the supply of wind, and the piece came to an abrupt end. A parallel story to this is told of the competition for the post of Court organist at Vienna, where a space of twenty-five minutes was allowed to each candidate for the development of a theme given by the judges; Bruckner got so interested that he had to be reminded that the allotted time had expired. Not even then did he cease, and after nearly one hour's playing he left off, greatly satisfied with himself, and entirely regardless of the effects of his performance upon those who were to adjudge the post. It is to the credit of these worthy gentlemen that they bestowed it on the unruly candidate.

In 1872 the distinguished critic, Dr. Hanslick,

wrote a glowing account of Bruckner's mass in F minor; his opinion of the composer and of the work changed completely in the course of time, and those who care to ferret out the weaknesses of eminent critics may be referred to the *Musikalisches Wochenblatt* for 1893, p. 280. It is not without significance, to those who are acquainted with the position of parties in the German musical world, that Bruckner's open allegiance to the cause of Wagner's music should have been made in the year after Hanslick's first article appeared. In 1873 Bruckner took the three symphonies, which then represented his work in that kind, to Bayreuth, and Wagner was so delighted with them that he willingly accepted the dedication of the third, in D minor. Its predecessor, in C minor, was performed for the first time at a concert organised by the composer for the closing of the Vienna exhibition of 1873. Wagner must have had reason to believe in Bruckner's powers, for he allowed the final chorus of "Die Meistersinger" to be given under his direction at a "Liedertafel" concert at Linz, several years before the comedy was performed as a whole.

In 1875 he was appointed University

Reader* at Vienna for musical theory and harmony; a pupil of his, Dr. R. Wallaschek, describes the admiration he excited in the students by working out extemporaneously fugues and canons, on themes given him at a moment's notice, with as much resource and clearness as if he had thought them over for a long time.

Such vogue as the composer has enjoyed in his own country did not fall to his share until 1884, when his seventh symphony, in E major, was given at Leipzig under Arthur Nikisch, at a concert in aid of the Wagner Memorial Fund. The adagio of the symphony is an elegy on Wagner, and the whole work is very decidedly Wagnerian in character; the theme introduced as the "Non confundar in aeternum" in a "Te Deum" of Bruckner's own, is a prominent feature in this adagio.† The work is throughout melodious and often effective, but it is so deeply

---

* A "Lector" is a teacher who has had no university education, and therefore cannot advance to a higher position in the university.

† The following note from the composer himself perhaps shows that the passage was at first intended for the words to which it was afterwards set, not at first conceived instrumentally :—" I composed the " Te

tinged with the Wagnerian influence that it can scarcely be regarded otherwise than as a reflection of his spirit, and the scherzo has been described as a mere transcription of the "Walkürenritt." Its popularity was rapid and extensive; Herr Richter conducted it at one of his London concerts in 1887, when it was received with favour, though with far less enthusiasm than it obtained in many towns of Germany. In 1891 another work of Bruckner's was given at the same concerts, viz., his symphony in D minor, No. 3, already referred to as being dedicated to Wagner. The scherzo, very certainly the best of the four movements, was to have been introduced to the English public years before, but Herr Richter found no opportunity of bringing it forward at his earlier seasons. The composer has here taken almost the identical theme of the first movement of Beethoven's Ninth Symphony for his own opening section;

Deum" in 1884, the symphony in 1883. Therefore I wrote the passage you refer to in the year 1883, just at the time of the death of our immortal master, who had predicted great things of me." He adds that his "Te Deum" is dramatically conceived, and that the trombones are supposed to reflect the sense of dread conveyed in the final words of the hymn.

the finale is cleverly constructed, but it cannot be said to have been very successful in London. Six months before, in Vienna, the repetition of the scherzo was so vigorously demanded, that Richter had to explain that it could not be repeated owing to the lateness of the hour. At the close of last year the same conductor, who is devoted to Bruckner's music, brought forward, also at Vienna, the eighth of his symphonies, in C minor; as its performance occupies an hour and a half, there is not room for much else in the programme, in a country where the musical digestion is better understood than it is with us. The adagio alone takes twenty-six minutes in performance, and yet the success of the work is said to have been beyond dispute. In the finale the composer has worked up contrapuntally the chief themes of the three preceding movements, and the instrumentation of the whole is very highly spoken of, even by those who least approve of the composer's "modern" tendencies.

The composer's chief production in the department of chamber music is a quintet in F major, which was brought forward on two occasions by the Hellmesberger quartet in Vienna with the greatest success. It is rumoured to be one of the most difficult works of its class in modern music, and is regarded apparently by both Wagnerians and anti-Wagnerians as an application of the Bayreuth master's methods to chamber music, a proceeding which can hardly be expected to be more successful than that of putting new wine into old bottles. Beside these works, a setting of Psalm cl. for soli, choir and orchestra, and a chorus, "Der Germannenzug," for male voices and brass instruments, are highly spoken of.

In character Bruckner is extremely straightforward, naïve, sincere and simple; in fact he seems hardly to belong to the present day, so complete is his disregard for the many *convenances* of Austrian musical society. It has been absolutely impossible to him to push his way onward in the world, and he has been content to let his symphonies remain unplayed some for a quarter of a century, without making any efforts to get a hearing for them. He is still very much of a rustic, and rather a "rough diamond" in many ways, and he is of those who hold that a musician's education is none the worse for not extending beyond the limits of his own art.

In 1886 he received the cross of the Franz Joseph Order, in 1890 the Upper Austrian Landtag bestowed upon him an annual pension of 400 gulden, and in 1891 the Vienna University made him Doctor of Philosophy *honoris causâ*.

An earlier and not less devoted Wagnerian than Bruckner, FELIX DRAESEKE, has scarcely as yet made the mark that might have been expected from a man of his high ideals and thoroughly artistic methods of working. With him, as with so many of the best of the unrecognised, an excessive habit of self-criticism has kept him from the position that a more unscrupulous man might have claimed, and has, of course, affected most materially the extent of his lists of works. A certain diffusion of interests, too, is partly responsible for the comparatively small number of his compositions, since he has contributed largely and with good results to the literature of music, and has gone somewhat deeply into the modern developments of pianoforte technique.

He was born October 7, 1835, at Coburg, where his father, the son of a once famous bishop of Magdeburg, was Court chaplain. He was educated at the "gymnasium" of his native town, and from 1852 to 1855 was a student at the Leipzig Conservatorium, studying with Richter, Hauptmann, and Rietz. In spite of the conservative tendencies of the school, he became a declared adherent of Wagner during his student days, being moved thereto by a performance of "Lohengrin" at Weimar in 1852, and one of "Tannhäuser" at Leipzig in 1853. Regarded in the light of the new music, and with this influence strong upon him, Beethoven's mass in D only confirmed him in his allegiance to the party of progress, and he undertook the analysis of Liszt's symphonic poems, brought out about 1857, executing the task with such literary ability and enthusiasm as to win the complete approval of the composer, whose acquaintance, with that of Bülow, he had been so fortunate as to make soon after leaving Leipzig for Berlin.

In the summer of 1857 he took up his abode in Dresden, and completed an opera, "König Sigurd," a work of which Liszt thought so highly that he got it accepted at Weimar and even rehearsed; just then, however, arose the storm over Cornelius's "Barbier von Bagdad," and on Liszt's resigning his post in consequence of the reception of that work, his young friend's opera naturally got "shelved." During his five years' stay in Dresden some of his works attracted a considerable degree of attention from the musicians of the advanced school; among these was a ballad for solo voice, "Helges Treue." His critical articles, contributed to the *Neue Zeitschrift für Musik*, had considerable influence at the time, and are now of some historical interest. At Löwenberg in Silesia, where he spent some months in the early part of 1862, he enjoyed the opportunity of hearing some of his compositions played by the private orchestra of the Prince of Hohenzollern-Hechingen. Shortly after this he went to Switzerland, where he lived until 1875, with the exception of nearly a year spent at Munich and an extensive foreign tour, settling down at Lausanne, and working at composition. Two symphonies, a pianoforte sonata, an "Adventlied" (op. 30), and part of a Requiem, were the chief productions of this period of his life. In 1873 the first of the symphonies, in G minor, op. 12, was given in Dresden, and in 1876 Draeseke returned to the Saxon capital, where he completed his second opera, "Herrat," a work which had to wait until 1892 for performance. His third opera, "Gudrun," was luckier in this respect, since it was given at Hanover in 1884. Meanwhile the Requiem was finished, and after being brought out at Leipzig in 1883 with very great success, it was given by many of the best choral societies in Germany. A third symphony, "Symphonia tragica," op. 40, was given in Dresden and Berlin in 1888, under Bülow. In 1880 Draeseke was appointed teacher of theory in the Rollfuss academy, and four years later he succeeded Wüllner as teacher of composition in the Dresden Conservatorium, a post which he still holds. His latest work of importance is a mass in F sharp minor, still in MS., given in Dresden and Leipzig in the winter of 1892. A new opera is in course of composition. Among the most prominent of his works, unmentioned above, are two "symphonic overtures" to "Das Leben ein Traum" and "Penthesilea," op. 45 and 50 respectively; "Jubiläums-Festmarsch," op. 54; Academic Overture (MS.); "Columbus," a cantata for soli, chorus and orchestra, op. 52; two string quartets; a quintet for piano, strings and horn, op. 48, and two curious sets of canons for pianoforte duet.

The composer has a decided gift of melody, though his themes are sometimes less "distinguished" in style than their treatment; he is more successful than most professed Wagnerians in the department of "absolute" music, though strong dramatic feeling is exhibited in his works for the stage. The ingenuity with which, in the "Domine" of his Requiem, he has brought in the chorale-tune, "Jesus meine Zuversicht," shows him to be a thoughtful and imaginative musician, and the whole work has considerable breadth and imaginative power; very few of his other works, however, seem to contain the elements of greatness in the strict sense of the word.

NEW PATHS (?)

JEAN LOUIS NICODÉ——RICHARD STRAUSS——HANS SOMMER——CYRILL KISTLER

WHEN Schumann wrote his famous article on the youthful Brahms, headed "Neue Bahnen," he seems almost to have discerned, as by a clear prophetic vision, the position which the young composer would ultimately reach; just as he had seen in the second published work of Chopin the imaginative power which, to ordinary observers, is by no means visible until a much later date. Such exceptional powers are not required in considering the claims of the leaders of the latest German school to be regarded as great composers, for all four of the men whose names stand at the head of this chapter have published far more important works than had been produced by either Chopin or Brahms at the time when Schumann first wrote about them. Still, it is impossible to declare with certain voice any one of the four to be the coming champion of music, unless it be first conceded that such a champion cannot be looked for anywhere but in Germany, and, therefore, that the best of the young Germans must of necessity be the future acknowledged master of the art for all the world. It is hard to believe that a time may possibly come when Germany will not contain the greatest master of the world's music; she has brought them forth in so regular a succession from the time of Bach and Handel until now, that the idea of her ceasing to bring them forth is hardly to be admitted, although the history of arts and of literature might teach us that the mere fact of the long series having been produced is an argument continually becoming more cogent in favour of its ceasing. The great Germans have curiously often come in pairs, as Bach and Handel, Haydn and Mozart, Beethoven and Schubert, Schumann and Mendelssohn; but from the four men who alone seem worthy of serious consideration in the present day, it were hard to fix upon two, or even upon one, who is fit, or who gives

JEAN LOUIS NICODÉ

promise of some day being fit, to assume the crown of music, and hand down the glorious line of German supremacy to yet another generation.

The first of the four, JEAN LOUIS NICODÉ, is wholly a German, in spite of the French form of his name; he was born at Jerczitz, near Posen, August 12, 1853. His father, a man of property, was a skilful amateur violinist, and on the loss of his fortune, some three years after the birth of his son, he removed to Berlin, where he turned his talent to good account. At the age of eight the boy began to learn the violin from his father, and three years afterwards a school friend gave him his first pianoforte lessons. His talent was already so remarkable that the organist of the St. Elizabeth Church in Berlin gave him free instruction in the organ, piano, and counterpoint. In 1869 he was admitted into the Neue Akademie der Tonkunst, and studied there for two years under Kullak for piano and Wüerst for theory. He was afterwards appointed one of the subordinate pianoforte masters in the same school, and from 1873 to 1876 served his time in the German army. On returning to Berlin he co-operated in conducting and accompanying at a series of "Monday Chamber Concerts," and during the three years of his tenure of this office he was studying composition with Kiel. On his return from a concert tour in Galicia and Roumania with Mariano Padilla and his wife, Mme. Désirée Artot, he went to Dresden as first pianoforte professor in the Conservatorium, a post which he retained until 1885, when he felt bound to resign it, owing to a violent difference of opinion with the council as to the value of Liszt's compositions for teaching purposes. The "last straw" was when Nicodé announced for performance at one of the Conservatorium concerts Liszt's own arrangement of his "Faust" symphony for two pianos; the directors, sheltering themselves behind the rule forbidding transcriptions, struck the number from the programme. In the autumn of the same year he started a most successful series of "Philharmonic Concerts" in Dresden, which he conducted for three years. Since 1888 he has devoted himself entirely to composition; in that year one of his most important works was brought out and made a considerable stir in different parts of Germany. "Das Meer" (op. 31), as it is called, may or may not have been suggested by

JEAN LOUIS NICODÉ

Rubinstein's "Ocean Symphony"; whether it is so or not, Nicodé's work cannot be reproached with any plagiarism further than that of name, and, to some extent, of form, since there are no less than seven movements in it. It is styled a "symphonic ode" and is cast for soli, male chorus, orchestra and organ. In style it is aggressively "modern," a piece of such uncompromising realism that, as a very eminent German musician expressed it, "one feels seasick as one listens to it." It shows very considerable powers of imagination and a strong feeling for the picturesque in music—qualities which appear also in a set of symphonic variations; in "Maria Stuart," a symphonic poem, and elsewhere. His orchestration is very often more noisy than skilful, and it may be surmised that the best of his numerous pianoforte works will ultimately take a higher position than anything he has written for the orchestra. In these he shows himself completely master of the instrument, and they have that delightful peculiarity (to pianists) of sounding far more difficult than they are—a peculiarity which distinguishes the music of many authors who are primarily virtuosi, or who, by choice or accident, are mainly writers for one instrument. As a teacher and an orchestral conductor he is excellent, and he has only done one thing which calls for censure—viz., the perpetration of an orchestral accompaniment to Chopin's Concert Allegro, op. 46, with the addition of a new "working-out section" of his own, consisting of more than seventy bars.

There is an important party in Germany, strong rather in influence than in mere numbers, which regards RICHARD STRAUSS as the coming man among the younger composers. As he is not yet thirty years old, it is unsafe to oppose too vehemently the opinion formed of him by these judges, although it may be permissible to point out that at the same age Brahms had produced, in the two serenades and the first sextet, works which stamped him as a genius of the highest order. Of course the standard of precocity varies constantly, and it is not always the infant prodigy who ultimately attains the highest rank; in different generations, too, development goes at different rates, so that a Mozart's lifework is done at an age when a Beethoven's genius has hardly declared itself. In Strauss' case it is fair to take what he has already accomplished as a test of his powers, since his early artistic growth was extraordinarily rapid, and he has had everything in his favour, except indeed the priceless boon of health. His father, Professor Fr. Strauss, was for many years considered to be the finest player of the waldhorn in Europe, and has for many years been chief horn-player in the Bavarian Court Band; his son was born at Munich, June 11, 1864, and music came to him as a natural inheritance. That he would listen with rapt attention to his father's practising, or be reduced to tears by the high notes of the violin, is not a sign that distinguishes him from many other babies of more or less sensitive nervous organisation; but to compose a three-part song at the age of six, after having had only the most rudimentary instruction on the piano up to that time, does strike one as an exceptional thing. It came about one Christmas time, as some children were singing round the Christmas tree, that he remarked, "I can do that, too!" and produced a composition he had written entirely without parental or other superintendence. It will be obvious to every musician that the wonder is, not that a child of six should invent little tunes, but that even an attempt at writing in parts should be made at that age. Shortly before this he was sent to the Volkschule, and at ten years old entered the "humanistische Gymnasium," as the main school for the study of "literæ humaniores" is oddly called. On completing the course there, he went, in 1882, to the university of his native city: for his father was quite aware of the primary value of a good general education—a somewhat rare degree of worldly wisdom in a professional musician. During his school-days music was, of course, not neglected; his school-books were degraded from their primary function as weapons of warfare to serve as material for jotting down musical ideas, since his mother had, happily, chanced to bind them in blank music-paper. During a French lesson, for instance, he wrote, in his fifteenth year, the scherzo of a string quartet, afterwards published as op. 2. Three years before this, during an illness, he had employed his time in writing a trio, which was played in the presence of Franz Lachner, and met with his approval. A piano sonata and other works dating from his school-days have also seen the light, but a chorus written to a Greek text, with orchestral accompaniments, and performed at a school concert, does not appear among his printed works. He was still at school when he wrote his first symphony in D minor, which was performed at a subscription concert by the Royal Band, and received with much favour. On the boy's repeated advances to the platform in answer to the applause, a stranger in the audience asked, in a voice that could be heard all over the room: " What has that boy got to do with the matter ? " "Oh, he's only the composer," was the reply. No fewer than eleven of his published works were actually printed while he was yet at school, among them concertos for violin and waldhorn —the latter a piece of enormous difficulty, obviously intended for his father's delectation. Yet he does not seem to have been forced on at all, nor even to have had any very first-rate musical training; he was under Herr W. Mayer, the Hofkapellmeister, for theory, and under Concertmeister Benno Walter for violin, until he met with Hans von Bülow, who was so much delighted with his serenade for thirteen wind-instruments, op. 7, that he gave it at Meiningen, and put it, together with the horn concerto, into the repertory of the famous band. On his return from a visit to Berlin (where a concert-overture of his was played with great success), at the close of his university career in 1883, the young composer betook himself to Frankfort, where, at the Raff Conservatorium he studied with Bülow, who at that time used to go to Frankfort for a month in every year. Bülow thought so much of Strauss' powers that he offered to take him to Meiningen as assistant conductor; almost immediately after the arrangement had been completed, Bülow's resignation of his appointment placed the splendid orchestra under the sole direction of Richard Strauss, a piece of good fortune almost without parallel in modern times. At his first appearance at Meiningen, Strauss played the D minor pianoforte concerto of Mozart to the conductor's complete satisfaction; not only was he compelled to play the solo part by heart, but the band were required to do the same. Another of the conductor's whims was to print the programme on a card, so as to avoid the rustle usually produced by a large audience all turning over their programmes at the same moment. While at Meiningen, Strauss wrote a pianoforte quartet, op. 13, which obtained the prize offered by the Berlin Tonkünstler-Verein, and in recognition of which he, the composer, received the "Verdienstkreuz für Kunst und Wissenschaft." A "Burleske" for piano and orchestra, and a set of variations and fugue for piano, written about this period, are not yet published. Another work written at this time, the symphony in F minor, op. 12, holds an important place in his life, as well as for its own sake; he was asked to conduct it at Munich, and the performance was so brilliantly successful that he was given, in August 1886, the post of conductor, under Levy, at the Munich Hoftheater. He conducted it in various musical centres of Germany, and twice in Milan, where he was made an honorary member of the "Società Quartetta," because of its success, and was, moreover, presented with a silver bâton by the members of the orchestra. His next work of importance, op. 16, "Aus Italien," a so-called symphonic fantasia for orchestra, was no doubt suggested by this visit to Italy; it is in some ways his most spontaneous and individual work, but the choice of theme for its last movement shows a strange want of taste, as well as of knowledge of the ordinary musical history of his time. For the song "Funiculìfuniculà" is not a traditional tune, nor is it possible to imagine how a cultivated musician should ever have mistaken it for one; it is far too vulgar to have sprung up, as national music always does, from the hearts of the people, or to be anything but a "composed" tune. As a consequence of this choice, the finale had to be left out when the work was given at one of Mr. Henschel's orchestral concerts a few years ago. He remained three years in Munich and wrote there his three "tone-poems,"—"Tondichtungen"—"Don Juan," op. 20; "Macbeth," op. 23, and "Tod und Verklärung," op. 24. In 1889 he was appointed second "Hofkapellmeister" at Weimar, a post he still holds with credit. He was chosen to conduct the performances of the Tonkünstler-Versammlung at Wiesbaden and Eisenach, an honour rarely conferred upon so young a man. In the winter of 1892 he was granted by the Grand Duchess of Weimar eight months' leave of absence, in order to recover his health, which had been broken by overwork; he returned lately from a tour in Greece, Italy, and Egypt, and is at present engaged in completing an opera, "Guntram," for which he has written his own libretto.

Strauss did not strike out a definite syle of his own until he had come, through Bülow, under the strong influence of the most modern music. In form and style his earlier compositions adhere to classical models, while his "tone-poems" and the like are uncompromisingly modern. Some of them show an excessive straining after originality, and some seem to have reached the ultimate point of ugliness. The composer's skill in orchestration is, perhaps, his best quality, though here he does not always exercise self-restraint: this is particularly the case with "Don Juan" and "Macbeth." The third of the tone-poems, "Tod und Verklärung," is a little apt to remind the hearer of "Tristan" and "Götterdämmerung": it has vivid imagination, is decidedly characteristic, and splendidly scored, but at the same time deficient in real musical inspiration. In what may be called the politics of music, he is not too rabid a radical to ignore such masters as Schumann and Brahms, and he has indeed been severely criticised by the Wagnerians for admitting works by these masters into his programmes at Weimar; not only that, but in a work for six-part choir and orchestra, set to a part of Goethe's "Wanderers Sturmlied," op. 14, given last May by the Allgemeine Deutsche Musikverein at Munich, he has, apparently, been influenced to a considerable extent by Brahms' "Schicksalslied" and the "Rhapsodie." A well-known critic ("C. A. B.") describes the work in the *Athenæum* of June 1, 1893, as being "enormously difficult and bravely attacked by the choir." He goes on to say, "Its effect as a broadly flowing stream of polyphonic vocal harmony against an elaborate and independent orchestral accompaniment was something quite unprecedented."

As a conductor Strauss is excellent, and his powers as a song-writer are very considerable. On the whole, he is one of the most interesting figures among the younger musicians of Germany, and it may, of course, be that those who regard him as a genius of the first order will be some day proved to be right. Time will show.

When Richard Strauss was born, HANS SOMMER was twenty-six years old, and yet he is properly to be considered among the younger composers, since his early life was passed in a very different sphere of work—as a professor of mathematics in the University of Göttingen. His full name is a somewhat formidable concern: "Hans Friedrich August Zincke genannt Sommer" is the way he himself writes it, and it is to be presumed that the last is a surname of choice. He was born at Brunswick, July 20, 1837, and his early predilections were from the first mathematical, rather than musical. Still, he began to learn the piano when he was ten years old, and during his residence at Göttingen, first as undergraduate, then as professor, he studied music with Julius Otto Grimm, and went in for it thoroughly, not merely in an amateur sort of way.

From 1875 to 1881 he was director of the "Technische Hochschule" in his native town, and in 1884 he retired altogether from public life as a mathematician, on account of ill health. In 1885 he married the daughter of the once famous "Kammersänger" Hill and went to live in Berlin, subsequently removing to Weimar, where he still lives. During a period of residence in Brunswick he was conductor of a concert society, and studied composition with a Herr Meves, making a first serious attempt at dramatic composition in a one-act opera, "Der Nachtwächter," a piece in the Lortzing manner, produced at Brunswick in 1865. He had become entitled to a pension as professor; and when he had once given up mathematics he took to composition in good earnest, and poured out an immense number of songs.

He has written many essays on musical as well as mathematical subjects; some of the former appeared in *Bayreuther Blätter*. He edited Georg Kaspar Schürman's opera, "Ludewig der Fromme," for the Gesellschaft für Musikforschung, by which it may be seen that his tastes in music are of the most eclectic kind. This characteristic is the first thing that strikes one in looking through the songs by which his name has become more or less famous in Germany. His published works in this form amount to nearly two hundred, so that in quantity, if not in quality, he bids fair some day to rival Schubert himself. The influence of Schubert is, perhaps, the oldest that he owns; for the most part, Franz, Schumann, Jensen, Brahms, seem to have been among his models, while throughout a tendency is perceived towards certain progressions that are characteristic of Wagner, and occasionally we meet with one of the stereotyped turns of musical phrases that we are apt to connect with Strauss' waltzes. A *leit-motiv* goes through the large number of songs from Wolff's "Rattenfänger," a set which contains the most bewitching of his songs, one called "Stelldichein" (an assignation). The vocal part, though entirely subordinate, is by no means ineffective, and the waltz, under cover of which the assignation is made, is perfectly irresistible. The next song in the set is scarcely less taking: "Am Waldteiche," as it is called, relates, in alternate lines of German and Latin, the adventure of a maiden who bathes in a woodland pool, and the contrasting treatment of the alternate lines is most happy and entirely appropriate. These are from the third set of op. 4, which contains also the Wagnerian "Herbst," and the melodious "Grabschrift." Op. 6, a set written to verses by the Queen of Roumania (Carmen Sylva), is, perhaps, more thoughtful than these, and some more elaborate "Balladen und Romanzen" are numbered opp. 8 and 11. A picturesque, if rather superficial, set of songs, mostly on Italian or Spanish subjects, called "Aus dem Süden," appears as op. 10. One of the most popular of Sommer's songs is "Frau Venus," from op. 9; and another, which deserves to be better known, is "Odysseus," from op. 11—a lyric of very remarkable beauty. Op. 12, "Werner's Lieder aus Welschland," and two pretty slumber songs, op. 15, are among his more recent works in the form in which his popularity has been gained.

Latterly he has been attempting the higher branches of vocal music: his opera "Lorelei," written to a libretto arranged by Gustav Gurski, from Wolff's poem, was given in Brunswick with great success on April 12, 1891, twenty-six years after his first opera was produced there. It is Wagnerian in its use of "leading-motives" and in many points of style, but the composer always has an eye to what is likely to be popular, and his decided gift of melody stands him in good stead in writing for the stage. One of Sommer's latest works is "Eliland; ein Sang am Chiemsee," written, after Stieler's poem, for declamation, tenor voice, and piano. It was given at the meeting of the Tonkünstler-Verein at Munich last summer, and is said to be a poetical little work, although it did not meet with unqualified approval from the musicians who were present. A comic opera, "Saint Foix," set to a very bright libretto by Hans von Wolzogen, has not yet been produced, but it promises to be a great success when it appears. It has been accepted for Munich, and Gura is to sing the title part.

It would be rash to count upon Sommer as the future representative of the great line of German song-writers, for the absence of any

CYRILL KISTLER

fixed ideal which is conspicuous in nearly all his compositions, clever as they are, is likely to gain him present popularity rather than permanent fame. Although his later songs show a decided increase in real worth, his uncertainty of artistic conviction is likely, sooner or later, to result in the usual lowering of the standard : for, even in Germany, popularity with the musical "masses" means a far greater degree of worldly prosperity than is to be gained by too firm an adherence to the highest aims.

Little more than a year after the death of Wagner there was brought out at Sondershausen, on March 20, 1883, a three-act opera, "Kunihild und der Brautritt auf Kynast," in which a certain section of the Wagnerian party discerned a worthy successor to the compositions of the master himself. Outside a small circle of ardent souls, the performance made no great noise in Germany, and it was only last year (1893) that the merits of the work were more widely discussed, in connection with its extremely successful revival at Würzburg on Febuary 24. The antecedents of the composer were not such as warranted his success. His previous works were mainly of a popular kind, such as polkamazurkas, marches, and those part-songs for male chorus in which the German student takes such lasting delight. Such wild oats as these need not, of course, stand as accusations against the artistic convictions of their sower; many a man who has done great things in after life has been compelled by circumstances to make a living by work confessedly far below his ideals, and there is now every reason to suppose that means will be found to enable the composer to pursue the high aims he has latterly professed. To become a recognised successor of a great master it is not enough to carry on precisely his method, applying it without alteration to new subjects. New developments must be made, or individuality exhibited in some direction or other; for, without this, the copyist's work is not only itself worthless, but it has the far more serious result of degrading the master's own work in the eyes of superficial observers. Now the art which Wagner developed during his life had this remarkable feature—that the career of a single man saw its inception, gradual advance, and completion: for it has of late years become pretty generally realised that this art, which may be called the art of music-drama, is entirely distinct from that of music alone, or from poetry alone, just as certainly as it is differentiated from that of scene-painting alone. In view of its extraordinary elaboration, and the certainty of effect with which it was used by its creator, it seems at least probable that it can reach no further point of development in its own direction, although it will be, and has already been, most fruitful of influence upon stage music of every school. If it were possible to remove Wagner and the body of his work from the history of music, the whole of the modern Italian school, from the later works of Verdi downwards, and most, if not all, of the healthiest schools of France and England, could never have existed, at all events in their present condition; but no development in Wagner's own direction has yet been even attempted. The first impression produced by the pianoforte score of " Kunihild " is that it contains nothing that has not already been said, and a great deal better said, by Wagner. The libretto, a cleverly constructed poem in alliterative verse on strictly Wagnerian lines, by Graf Sporck (the author's name has only lately been made public), deals with a legend that is full of opportunities for closely imitating the manner of the Bayreuth master. By an elaborate system of "leading-motives" and the use of harmonic progressions that arrested attention, whether for praise or blame, when they first appeared in the later works of Wagner, a copy has been produced that might quite easily pass for a work of Wagner's, were it not that in the various scenes in which short choruses are introduced a sudden and entirely uncalled-for change is made from the declamatory and passionate style to part-writing of the tamest description, suggesting that the composer's earlier style has not, after all, been quite abandoned. The opera may be effective on the stage, grateful to the singers, and suggestive to thoughtful hearers, but if it stood alone the prediction that Wagner's life-work would be carried on by CYRILL KISTLER would seem to rest on anything but a solid foundation. At the same time, it is undeniable that, with no small powers of invention, he has acquired a very remarkable mastery over means of expression; granting the strong influence of the older master, the music is appropriate to the characters of the drama, and its various situations are grasped with very decided ability. The composition of this work did not occupy him long; in fact, three months were all he spent upon it, not including the scoring.

CYRILL KISTLER

Born in 1848, at Grossaitingen, near Augsburg, he was early left an orphan and adopted by his grandfather, a shoemaker, who encouraged such love for music as he displayed; at eight years old he was a choirboy, and could play the flute. A first intention of preparing him for holy orders being abandoned, he was educated for the career of a schoolmaster, and from 1867 to 1875 he taught in various schools, studying music only as a recreation; not till 1876, when he entered the Munich Conservatorium, did he receive anything more than the usual amount of musical teaching that every schoolboy in Germany receives in the natural order of things. Under Rheinberger, Franz Lachner, Wüllner, and other teachers, he remained here for two years, subsequently becoming a private pupil of Lachner, who did not at all approve of the Wagnerian tendencies which, even then, had declared themselves. The time between the completion of his studies and the commencement of his career as a dramatic composer was spent in the composition of various works of small calibre. It is easily credible that he pondered the themes, etc., of "Kunihild" long before the winter of 1881-2, when it was composed; the scoring was not completed until February,

1883, and by a curious coincidence the day of its completion was the death-day of Richard Wagner. By this time he had been appointed teacher of musical theory in the Conservatorium at Sondershausen; two years later, Kistler moved to Kissingen, whence he published some not very well-judged contributions to musical literature, some of them called forth by the refusal of a certain manager to bring out his opera unless the composer paid him £750 for the privilege. It is certainly not by literary work or criticism that Kistler's name will be known, and very few of the numbers of his "Tagesfragen" (questions of the day)—a brochure of somewhat spasmodic character, both in its matter and in the irregularity of its appearance—are worth reading. So far as Kistler is to be judged by works already brought out, including many pieces of dance-music, no doubt written for the fashionable world of the watering-place, and several musicianly marches (notably one on the death of Wagner, in which the themes of Beethoven's march in A flat minor, and of Siegfried's death-march, are combined with good effect), the position claimed for him by a small band of admirers seems hardly justified. There have been issued, however, from the composer's publishing office at Kissingen—for he is to some extent his own publisher—a pair of operatic scores which have far greater individuality than appears in his first opera. The first, a musical comedy, based on Kotzebue's "Eulenspiegel," is entirely free from any debt to Wagner; it shows in every scene a distinct gift of comic power, and its popularity, in Germany at least, seems to be assured as soon as it is brought out. The fatuous opening theme, with its resemblance to the silly tune known as the "Chopsticks" waltz, exactly suits the character of the chief personage, the apprentice, half stupid, half mischievous, who disobeys every order of his master, though strictly fulfilling the letter of his injunctions. The working up of this theme in the overture, and the really masterly way in which the fun is kept up in the music, as well as the power of characterisation displayed throughout, are far more hopeful signs for the future fame of Kistler than anything to be found in "Kunihild." In "Baldur's Tod," the third of Kistler's operas, we are again in surroundings that suggest Wagner; many of the personages are identical with those in "Der Ring des Nibelungen," and some of them are true to the characters Wagner has given them. The Odin of the younger composer is quite as much given to discoursing at enormous length on things in general as his prototype, the Wotan of the Cycle. For all that, the work is well handled, and, even on a perusal of the piano score, reveals many beautiful points; the choral parts, again, are far more homogeneous with the rest of the music than is the case in the earlier work, and, in spite of many superficial resemblances to the trilogy, which, after all, can scarcely be avoided, the music has a character of its own, and a very beautiful character too. In August of last year the circumstance that a monk plays the part of villain in the earlier opera drew forth the wrath, not only of the local press, but of the Church, one preacher going so far as to denounce the performance from the pulpit.

The composer lives a quiet life, in surroundings excellently adapted to the production of worthy works of art. In person he is described, in a recent number of *The Meister* (to which the reader may be referred for further information), as about 5 ft. 10 in. in height, "large-boned, slightly stooping, with strongly-marked and regular features, keen dark eyes, rhetorical lips, and a forehead and shock of hair like Beethoven's." A portrait prefixed to *Baldur's Tod* bears this out, though it **does** not throw much light on the epithet "rhetorical."

The art which Wagner brought to perfection—the art, that is to say, of the music-drama—has lain dormant since his death; one is tempted to liken it to the sword Nothung, buried **to** the hilt in the ash-stem by Wotan, the world's wanderer. Will Kistler's be the hand to draw it forth?

www.ingramcontent.com/pod-product-compliance
Lightning Source LLC
Chambersburg PA
CBHW022021240426
43667CB00042B/1045